MODERN HUMANITIES RESEARCH ASSOCIATION
LIBRARY OF MEDIEVAL WELSH LITERATURE

General Editors
NERYS ANN JONES
ERICH POPPE

A SELECTION OF EARLY WELSH SAGA POEMS

Edited by
Jenny Rowland

LIBRARY OF MEDIEVAL WELSH LITERATURE

Already Published

Welsh Court Poems
edited by Rhian M. Andrews (2007)
(available from University of Wales Press)

Selections from Ystorya Bown o Hamtwn
edited by Erich Poppe and Regine Reck (2009)
(available from University of Wales Press)

Early Welsh Gnomic amd Nature Poetry
edited by Nicolas Jacobs (2012)
(available from www.medwelsh.mhra.org.uk)

Historical Texts from Medieval Wales
edited by Patricia Williams (2012)
(available from www.medwelsh.mhra.org.uk)

A SELECTION OF EARLY WELSH SAGA POEMS

Edited by
Jenny Rowland

Modern Humanities Research Association
2014

Published by

The Modern Humanities Research Association,
1 Carlton House Terrace
London SW1Y 5AF
United Kingdom

© *The Modern Humanities Research Association, 2014*

Jenny Rowland has asserted her right under the Copyright, Designs and Patents Act 1988 to be identified as the author of this work. Parts of this work may be reproduced as permitted under legal provisions for fair dealing (or fair use) for the purposes of research, private study, criticism, or review, or when a relevant collective licensing agreement is in place. All other reproduction requires the written permission of the copyright holder who may be contacted at rights@mhra.org.uk.

First published 2014

ISBN (hardback) 978-1-907322-63-1
ISBN (paperback) 978-1-907322-75-4

Copies may be ordered from www.medwelsh.mhra.org.uk

CONTENTS

Acknowledgements		vii
Abbreviations		ix
Bibliography		xi
Introduction		xv
Texts		
I	'Gwên a Llywarch' and 'Marwnad Gwên'	1
II	'Cân yr Henwr'	4
III	Canu Heledd	6
IV	'Llym Awel'	16
Notes		21
Glossary		75

ACKNOWLEDGMENTS

I would like to thank the editors of the series for their patience, encouragement, suggestions and corrections. In the latter stages my University College Dublin post-graduate students served as 'guinea pigs' for the edition. They provided valuable feedback, and also went beyond the call of duty to check the glossary and notes for errors. Many thanks, then, to Adrian Doyle, Juliana Roost and Christopher Walker. I must also thank Prof. Marged Haycock for her observations, corrections and many other kindnesses during the writing of this work. Inconsistencies and errors which remain are due to my own failings.

ABBREVIATIONS

adj.	adjective
adv.	adverb
c.	century
cf.	compare
conj.	conjunction
dat.	dative
f.	feminine
fig.	figurative
fut.	future
imperf.	imperfect
Ir.	Irish
L.	Latin
lit.	literally
m.	masculine
MnW	Modern Welsh
ms.	manuscript
mss.	manuscripts
MW	Middle Welsh
n.	noun
neg.	negative
obj.	object
OIr	Old Irish
OW	Old Welsh
perf.	perfect
pl.	plural
prep.	preposition
pres.	present
pret.	preterite
sg.	singular
vn	verbal noun
BBCS	*Bulletin of the Board of Celtic Studies*
CA	*Canu Aneirin*, ed. Ifor Williams
CBT	*Cyfres Beirdd y Tywysogion*

CLlH	*Canu Llywarch Hen*, ed. Ifor Williams
CMCS	*Cambrian Medieval Celtic Studies* (1981–1992 *Cambridge Medieval Celtic Studies*)
CO	*Culhwch and Olwen: An Edition and Study of the Oldest Arthurian Tale*, ed. Rachel Bromwich and D. Simon Evans
EWSP	*Early Welsh Saga Poetry*, ed. Jenny Rowland
GMW	A *Grammar of Medieval Welsh*, D. Simon Evans
GPC	*Geiriadur Prifysgol Cymru*
NLW 4973B	National Library of Wales Ms. 4973B
PT	*Poems of Taliesin*, ed. Ifor Williams
SC	*Studia Celtica*
TYP	*Trioedd Ynys Prydein*, ed. Rachel Bromwich
ZCP	*Zeitschrift für celtische Philologie*

BIBLIOGRAPHY

BARTRUM, P. C., ed. *Early Welsh Genealogical Tracts* (Cardiff, 1966).
——, *A Welsh Classical Dictionary* (Aberystwyth, 1993).
BREEZE, ANDREW, 'Old English *franca*, "spear": Welsh *ffranc*', *Notes and Queries* 236 (1991), pp. 98–99.
BROMWICH, RACHEL and D. SIMON EVANS, eds, *Culhwch and Olwen: An Edition and Study of the Oldest Arthurian Tale* (Cardiff, 1992).
BROMWICH, RACHEL, ed., *Trioedd Ynys Prydein*, 2nd edition (Cardiff, 1978).
CHARLES-EDWARDS, T. M., '*Mi a dynghaf dynghed* and related problems', in *Hispano-Gallo-Brittonica: Essays in honour of Professor Ellis Evans*, ed. Joseph Eska *et al.* (Cardiff, 1995), pp. 1–15.
——, *Wales and the Britons 350–1064* (Oxford, 2013).
Cyfres Beirdd y Tywysogion, 7 volumes, general editor R. Geraint Gruffydd (Caerdydd, 1991–1996).
CYNDDELW, 'Gwelygorddau Powys', ed. Nerys Ann Jones and Ann Parry Owen, *Gwaith Cynddelw Brydydd Mawr I*, CBT, Vol. III, pp. 113–27.
DAY, JENNY, 'Shields in Welsh Poetry up to c. 1300: Decoration, Shape and Significance', SC 45 (2011), pp. 27–52.
EVANS, D. SIMON, *A Grammar of Middle Welsh* (Dublin, 1964).
FORD, PATRICK K., 'Llywarch, Ancestor of Welsh Princes', *Speculum* 45.3 (1970), pp. 442–50.
——, *The Poetry of Llywarch Hen* (Berkeley, 1974).
——, 'A Highly Important Pig', in *Celtic Language, Celtic Culture: A Festschrift for Eric P. Hamp*, ed. A.T.E. Matonis and Daniel F. Melia (Van Nuys, Calif., 1990), pp. 292–304.
Geiriadur Prifysgol Cymru (Caerdydd, 1950–2002). A searchable version is available online: http://www.welsh-dictionary.ac.uk/
GRIFFEN, T. D., 'Generic consonant correspondences in *Canu Aneirin*', *Journal of Celtic Linguistics* 2 (1994), 93–105.
HAMP, ERIC, '*Culhwch* the Swine', ZCP 41 (1986), pp. 257–58.
HAYCOCK, MARGED, *Blodeugerdd Barddas o Ganu Crefyddol Cynnar* (Llandybïe, 1994).
——, 'Hanes Heledd hyd yma', in *Gweledigaethau: Cyfrol Deyrnged yr Athro Gwyn Thomas*, ed. J. W. Davies (Abertawe, 2007), pp. 29–60.
——, *Legendary Poems from the Book of Taliesin* (Aberystwyth, 2007).
HIGLEY, SARAH L. *Between Languages: The Uncooperative Text in Early Welsh and Old English Nature Poetry* (University Park: Pennsylvania, 1994).
Historia Brittonum, ed. and trans. John Morris (London, 1980).
HUWS, DANIEL, *Medieval Welsh Manuscripts* (Cardiff, 2000).
ISAAC, G. R., *Yr Hengerdd: Mynegeiriau Cyflawn* [CD] (Aberystwyth, 2001).

—— and SIMON RODWAY, *Rhyddiaith Gymraeg o Lawysgrifau'r 13eg Ganrif: Testun Cyflawn* [CD] (Caerdydd, 2002).
JACKSON, KENNETH H., *Early Welsh Gnomic Poems* (Cardiff, 1960).
JACOBS, NICOLAS, 'Celtic Saga and the Contexts of Old English Elegiac Poetry', *Études Celtiques* 26 (1989), 95–142.
——, ed., *Early Welsh Gnomic and Nature Poetry* (London, 2012).
——, 'Sylwadau pellach ar ?*im bluch* (=*ymlwch*) "yn foel"', *Llên Cymru* 21 (1998), pp. 162–5.
JARMAN, A. O. H., *The Cynfeirdd: early Welsh poets and poetry* (Cardiff, 1981).
——, 'The heroic ideal in early Welsh poetry', in *Beiträge zur Indogermanistik und Keltologie*, ed. W. Meid (Innsbruck, 1967), pp. 193–211.
——, *Llyfr Du Caerfyrddin gyda Rhagymadrodd, Nodiadau Testunol a Geirfa* (Cardiff, 1982).
——, ed., 'Saga Poetry — The Cycle of Llywarch Hen', in *A Guide to Welsh Literature Vol. 1*, ed. A. O. H. Jarman and G. R. Hughes (Cardiff, 1992), pp. 81–97.
JONES, NERYS ANN, 'Y Gogynfeirdd a'r Englyn', in *Beirdd a Thywysogion: Barddoniaeth Llys yng Nghymru, Iwerddon a'r Alban*, ed. Morfydd E. Owen and Brynley F. Roberts (Caerdydd, 1996), pp. 288–301.
——, 'Hengerdd in the Age of the Poets of the Princes', in *Beyond Gododdin: Dark Age Scotland in Medieval Wales*, ed. Alex Woolf (St. Andrews, 2013), pp. 41–80.
JONES, THOMAS, ed., 'The Black Book of Carmarthen "Stanzas of the Graves"', *Proceedings of the British Academy* 53 (1967), pp. 97–137.
KOCH, JOHN T., *Celtic Culture: A Historical Encyclopedia* (Oxford, 2006).
LLOYD-JONES, J., *Geirfa Barddoniaeth Gynnar Cymraeg* (Caerdydd, 1931–1963).
MAC CANA, PROINSIAS, 'Notes on the Combination of Prose and Verse in Early Irish Narrative', in *Early Irish Literature: Media and Communication*, ed. S. N. Tranter and H. L. C. Tristram (Tübingen, 1989), pp. 125–48.
——, 'Prosimetrum in Insular Celtic Literature', in *Prosimetrum: Crosscultural Perspectives on Narrative in Prose and Verse*, ed. Joseph Harris and Karl Reichl (Woodbridge, 1997), pp. 99–130.
MCKEE, HELEN, *The Cambridge Juvencus manuscript glossed in Latin, Old Welsh, and Old Irish: Text and Commentary* (Aberystwyth, 2000).
——, 'Scribes and Glosses from Dark Age Wales: The Cambridge Juvencus Manuscript', *CMCS* 39 (2000), pp. 1–22.
ROBERTS, RICHARD GLYN, *Diarhebion Llyfr Coch Hergest* (Aberystwyth, 2013).
RODWAY, SIMON, 'Absolute forms in the poetry of the Gogynfeirdd: functionally obsolete archaisms or working system?', *Journal of Celtic Linguistics* 7 (1998), pp. 63–84.
——, 'A Datable Development in Medieval Literary Welsh', *CMCS* 36 (1998), pp. 71–94.
——, *Dating Medieval Welsh Literature: Evidence from the Verbal System* (Aberystwyth, 2013).
——, 'Two developments in medieval literary Welsh and their implications for dating texts', in *Yr hen iaith: studies in early Welsh*, ed. Paul Russell (Aberystwyth, 2003), pp. 67–74.
ROWLAND, JENNY, *Early Welsh Saga Poetry: A Study and Edition of the Englynion* (Cambridge, 1990).

——, 'The Family of Cyndrwyn and Cynddylan', BBCS 29 (1981), pp. 526-27.
——, 'Genres', in *Early Welsh Poetry: Studies in the Book of Aneirin*, ed. Brynley F. Roberts (Aberystwyth, 1988), pp. 179-208.
——, 'The Manuscript Tradition of the Red Book *Englynion*', SC 18/19 (1983-1984), pp. 79-95.
——, 'Old Welsh *franc*: An Old English borrowing?', CMCS 26 (1993), pp. 21-25.
——, 'The Prose Setting of the Early Welsh *Englynion Chwedlonol*', *Ériu* 36 (1985), pp. 29-43.
Russell, Paul, 'The *englyn* to St Padarn Revisited', CMCS 63 (2012), pp. 1-14.
——, 'Scribal (In)consistency in Thirteenth-century South Wales: The Orthography of the Black Book of Carmarthen', SC 43 (2009), pp. 135-74.
Sharpe, Richard, 'Claf Abercuawg and the voice of Llywarch Hen', *Studia Celtica* 43 (2009), pp. 95-121.
Sims-Williams, Patrick, 'The Death of Urien', CMCS 32 (1996), pp. 25-56.
——, '"Is it fog or smoke or warriors fighting?": Irish and Welsh parallels to the *Finnsburg* fragment', BBCS 27 (1978), pp. 505-14.
——, 'The Provenance of the Llywarch Hen Poems: a Case for Llan-gors, Brycheiniog', CMCS 26 (1993), pp. 27-63.
Tristram, Hildegard L. C., 'Early Modes of Insular Expression', in *Saints, Sages and Storytellers: Celtic Studies in Honour of James Carney*, ed. Donnchadh Ó Corráin et al. (Maynooth, 1989), pp. 427-48.
——, 'The Early Insular Elegies: ITEM ALIA', in *Celtic Linguistics: Ieithyddiaeth Geltaidd*, ed. Martin J. Ball et al. (Amsterdam, 1990), 343-61.
Watkins, T. Arwyn, 'The Descriptive Predicative in Old and Middle Welsh', in *Hispano-Gallo-Brittonica: Essays in honour of Professor Ellis Evans*, ed. Joseph F. Eska et al. (Cardiff, 1995), pp. 278-303.
—— and Proisias Mac Cana, 'Cystrawennau'r Cyplad mewn Hen Gymraeg', BBCS 18 (1958-1960), pp. 1-25.
Welsh, Andrew, 'Branwen, Beowulf and the Tragic Peaceweaver Tale', *Viator* 22 (1991), pp. 1 13.
Williams, Ifor, ed. *Canu Llywarch Hen*, 2nd. edn (Caerdydd, 1953).
——, 'The Juvencus Poems', in *The Beginnings of Welsh Poetry*, ed. R. Bromwich (Cardiff, 1972), pp. 89-121.
——, *Lectures on Early Welsh Poetry* (Dublin, 1944).
——, 'The poems of Llywarch Hên' (Sir John Rhys Memorial Lecture), *Proceedings of the British Academy* 18 (1934 for 1932), pp. 209-302. Reprinted in *The Beginnings of Welsh Poetry*, ed. Rachel Bromwich (Cardiff, 1972), pp. 122-54.
——, ed., *Poems of Taliesin*. English version by J. E. Caerwyn Williams (Dublin, 1968).
Williams, J. E. Caerwyn, 'Nodiadau Testunol', BBCS 21 (1964), pp. 26-30.

INTRODUCTION

In many ways the saga *englynion* are ideal introductory texts for students of early medieval Welsh poetry. While it is common to begin with the earliest praise poetry, those poems present numerous textual and interpretative problems. The texts of the saga *englynion* are generally well-preserved and their dating and origin less controversial. The style is relatively direct and unelaborate, unlike the obscure and archaic style of the poetry from the period of the Poets of the Princes. The poems often have wider appeal for modern readers than praise poetry or other genres such as gnomic and religious verse. Nevertheless, to understand complete poems and cycles in context additional non-textual information is required. This introduction will deal broadly with the most important points. Some additional information can be found in the notes. Fuller discussion can be found in *Early Welsh Saga Poetry* and in works for additional reading listed in the bibliography.

Prose-verse Composition

Many difficulties in interpretation arise from the genre. Saga verse has been preserved without its original context in the Welsh story-telling tradition, however narrowly or broadly we define that context. The close connection of the poetry to story is essential for understanding the somewhat jumbled mass of poetry as it has come down to us in the manuscripts, and also lies at the heart of its long-lasting appeal. The few titles in the manuscripts suggest that the poets were speaking through characters from stories, and that these rubrics were given as a guide to placing the poems in a narrative context probably well-known to their original audiences. This knowledge was lost, along with much other knowledge of Welsh story-telling, by the end of the Middle Ages, and most of the poetry was ascribed to Llywarch Hen, a leading character in some of it. In the 1930s Ifor Williams reinterpreted the poetry as belonging to monologues or dialogues in character from saga, using comparisons with other early literature. This was followed by his painstaking reconstruction of the cycles and stories, and his masterful edition of the majority of the poetry in 1935.

Ifor Williams believed the poetry was the remains of extensive prose-verse sagas, with only the poetry, because it was invariable, given preservation in writing. He argued that the prose elements would have been long and involved, resembling the *Mabinogi* (which has a scattering of verses) or *The Táin* in early

Irish. Rather than postulate that Welsh storytelling changed drastically over a relatively short period, virtually abandoning earlier poetic elements, it is possible that the saga *englynion* were a separate type of composition. The stories appear to be different, dealing with historical figures of the heroic age rather than euhemerized gods of the pre-Christian past. The saga characters face realistic dilemmas, and magic and wonder have no obvious role in the reconstructions. Most importantly, the focus would appear to be on the character's reaction in the poetry to events rather than on relating a series of exciting plot elements.

This suggests the prose element for the *englynion* would have been more limited, and also that the setting could vary from saga to saga, and even from performance to performance. The extracts from the cycles selected for this book demonstrate this. Llywarch Hen is connected in the genealogies to the chief heroes of the men of the old North, but it is likely his story was shaped in Wales. The central, defining episode of his cycle is the inciting of Gwên, his last surviving son out of twenty-four, to unwise behaviour in battle, and Llywarch's subsequent grief when he finally realizes what he has done (I). The story may be the creation of the poet based on little more than his epithet, *hen* 'old'.[1] The consequences also lead to his famous lament in old age, which one can easily imagine also performed effectively apart from a full rendition of the tale (II). It is clear that composition continued quite late, codifying Llywarch's other sons, and linking them with local heroes; an example can be found in the Black Book poem included in this volume, 'Llym Awel' (IV). Some non-antiquarian poems set chronologically before the episode with Gwên show Llywarch's typical treatment of his sons. They could be earlier, but they may well have been composed after the core. There is also the problem of the link made to another complex *englynion* cycle about Llywarch's cousin, Urien.[2] It is clear that the poetry, which is not in chronological order in the manuscripts, cannot represent the remains of a single redaction of Llywarch's story at any given date, and new material may have been added in reference to the well-known story of Llywarch and his sons rather than being incorporated into a full retelling.[3]

The three poems in I and II selected for this volume present the core tale. The debate between Gwên and Llywarch resembles a drama. The *marwnad* (elegy) for Gwên and Llywarch's lament in old age concentrate on Llywarch's character development and emotional response. While some introductory prose would have been necessary, only a sentence or two could have sufficed, and most of the essential story elements could be gathered from the poetry and its performance.

---

[1] See Patrick K Ford., 'Llywarch, Ancestor of Welsh Princes', *Speculum* 45.3 (1970), pp. 442–50.
[2] On the development of the story of Llywarch in Wales and the link to the legends about the men of the Old North see EWSP, pp. 7–11; Patrick Sims-Williams, 'The Provenance of the Llywarch Hen Poems: A Case for Llan-gors, Brycheiniog', CMCS 26 (1993), pp. 27–63 and 'The Death of Urien', CMCS 32 (1996), pp. 25–56. Richard Sharpe reconsiders the manuscript context of the poems in 'Claf Abercuawg and the Voice of Llywarch Hen', *Studia Celtica* 43 (2009), pp. 95–121.
[3] Discussed further in Jenny Rowland, 'The Prose Settling of the Early Welsh *Englynion Chwedlonol*', *Ériu* 36 (1985), pp. 29–43.

Canu Heledd (III) also has a narrator and cast of characters drawn from an historical milieu. Heledd is said to be the sister of Cynddylan, an early seventh-century king of Powys, who appears in a few other early sources.[4] The first 65 stanzas in the manuscripts are tightly linked in time and sequence. The remaining stanzas consist of short poems reflecting some narrative content as well as more antiquarian type verses.[5] In these verses some time has elapsed since Cynddylan's fall, although on the whole the narrator, theme and mood continue to be the same. With the first part we could envision the verse was taken from a redaction of the story of Heledd with prose interludes omitted in the writing down. The challenge for the theory that the tale once had extensive prose, however, is the fact that considerable and exciting events have clearly taken place before the start of the surviving poetry, while very little happens in terms of narrative after the point where it begins. The interest in the cycle lies in the emotional response of Heledd to the downfall of her brother and destruction of Powys. The balance of prose versus poetry, and recounting of events versus introspection would be extremely uneven if the poetry had been preceded by extensive prose. In this case, it would seem that the poet shaped his *englyn* saga with reference to a tale or series of tales which were already well-known to audiences of the time and which would require only a minimum of prose introduction. Verses after 65 include shorter sequences and epigrams in keeping with the themes of the opening, but the relationship of 'Caranfael' to the story of the opening cycle is unclear, and some other verses may be intrusive.

'Llym Awel' (IV) is the only work in this book not taken from the White Book and Red Book collection of *englynion*. It is one of several saga poems found in the Black Book of Carmarthen, most of them single poems rather than cycles. This enigmatic work is probably an exception to this single poem pattern, containing at least two related pieces, and other less obviously related material. This may explain its patchy editorial record and comparative neglect. The first 24 stanzas and one further stanza were edited by Kenneth Jackson in *Early Welsh Gnomic Poems* (1935), which entertained a saga context for the opening, but primarily stressed the similarities to gnomic nature poetry.[6] Ifor Williams's edition gave only what he saw as the relevant lines up to stanza 22, but edited the remaining stanzas. He discusses the poem briefly in *Canu Llywarch Hen*, teasing

---

[4] There is a *marwnad* to him in *awdl* metre which survives in a late manuscript; for the text and translation see EWSP, pp. 174–89. His name inexplicably is omitted in the genealogies of the Cyndrwynin; Jenny Rowland, 'The Family of Cyndrwyn and Cynddylan', BBCS 29 (1981), pp. 526–27.

[5] Antiquarian verses added to cycles are often single stanzas. The chief intent seems not to advance or complement a story, but to record information: on heroes, genealogy, grave sites, places, gnomes and proverbs, historical titbits, etc. Apart from scattered stanzas, there are longer poems of this type, for instance 'Englynion y Beddau' ('The Stanzas of the Graves'). Some dialogues which resemble saga poems also seem to be primarily intended to present information; see below.

[6] The recent edition by Nicolas Jacobs, *Early Welsh Gnomic and Nature Poetry* (London, 2012) also omits some of the closing material.

out a theme from the human gnomes and suggesting there was a dialogue in the opening stanzas hidden under 'filler lines' of nature description. Unlike the other cycles he does not add editorial titles to the proposed sections. 'Llym Awel' is also related to the Llywarch cycle by a *marwnad* to Mechydd ap Llywarch, a verse mentioning another son, and verses found elsewhere in the Black Book under the title 'The Names of the Sons of Llywarch Hen'. There is undoubtedly some sort of narrative context behind the opening and the following dialogue which takes place during an expedition to rescue Owain Rheged. The relationship of these two poems to the *marwnad* for Mechydd is less clear, although details in the poem suggest there may once have been a tale about him. It also seems that the strong gnomic and nature element in the beginning has led to interpolations of originally unrelated gnomic verses.

The mixed material in 'Llym Awel' is a reminder that the saga-type verse contains far more variety than is covered here, a variety which in some cases may have created more and more distance from a saga retelling of a story in verse and even limited prose. The narrator persona may in cases have been a new or anonymous creation of the poet, in order to explore themes. A dialogue could be used for antiquarian purposes, with one rather colourless character asking questions of the target character. The dialogue question and answer could also serve the purpose of religious instruction while the emotional voice of a persona sometimes can be seen adding interest to gnomic and religious verse.[7] The metre itself and some of the metrical techniques of the *englynion* sequences also encourage the melding of genres. Disparate matter could be covered in a single short stanza, linked by theme, or by rather mechanical use of verbal repetition or question and answer.

Interpretation

Interpretation of the poems edited here is largely covered in the notes, and given the many uncertainties and ambiguities the reader is encouraged to explore other possible ways of placing the poems in context. Poems I, II and IV all explore the limits of heroism in a way not appropriate to bardic praise poetry, giving a more balanced picture of the warrior ethos. Llywarch Hen in I and II seems to embody the extreme stance of the heroic warrior. He has taunted his sons with the accomplishments of his own glorious youth, contrasting it to their less heroic deeds. Whether or not his own picture of his past is correct (his son, Gwên, seems to challenge it obliquely), the purpose of his taunting is to incite his sons to more extreme heroism and then bask in their reflected glory. Given the extreme heroic nature of praise poetry we might expect Llywarch to be a model for heroic society,

---

[7] Jenny Rowland, 'Genres', in *Early Welsh Poetry: Studies in the Book of Aneirin*, ed. Brynley F. Roberts (Aberystwyth, 1988), pp. 179–208; EWSP, pp. 276–91.

but instead see an inadequate man who only wakes to his errors with the death of his final son. It would have been far better and fairer for his sons to have decided for themselves how far to push their heroic vows. Both Llywarch's *marwnad* for Gwên and his lament in old age acknowledge that his lonely fate is largely of his own making.[8]

The typical picture of the older warrior cautioning the younger against too extreme vows which could lead to loss of honour or unnecessary loss of life is turned on its head by Llywarch. In the opening part of IV we may have depicted the proper course of decision for the seasoned warrior. The narrator questions whether his arguments for avoiding a dangerous and unseasonal mission are valid or masking cowardly reluctance. The process of mindful decision is followed, although in the end the speaker elects to depend on the ability of a brave warrior to avoid fate. These poems in character allow us to see that the ideal hero is expected to be not simply brave, but also to exercise appropriate forethought, an example of the *topos* of *fortitudo et sapientia* found in other heroic literatures.

The lament of Llywarch in old age (II) forms a fitting ending to the portrayal of how his quest for glory for his sons and himself led to disaster, and ultimately a lonely old age. Much of the poem, however, dwells on the indignities and bodily infirmities of old age, and as such has universal application. We see a man literally marginalized, little comforted by thoughts of his warrior past, and out of harmony with both mankind and nature. The final stanzas reveal the reason why Llywarch's old age is particularly bleak: the loss of his sons through his own misguided goading. Like the *marwnad* to Gwên it shows his character has developed, forced by tragedy to question his deepest values and in turn forcing the audience to also reconsider their assumptions.

The role of fate is another aspect which runs through the poems here. There may not be a single attitude. The final verse of Llywarch's lament on his old age suggests the old man's fate was fixed from the day of his birth (II.21). The treatment of his sons, however, would seem to indicate that he is largely responsible for his own troubles, and that his fortune could have been much different if he had been *dedwydd* (I.20c), a more complex idea than simply 'lucky'. Gwên and his other sons did not survive their fights because of their father's tongue (I.29). His innate character as quarrelsome, overly desirous of fame and unconcerned for his own offspring ultimately led to his lonely fate.

Among the gnomes and proverbial statements which seem to present the narrator debating the wisdom of an expedition in IV are two relating to fate. The truism that death ultimately cannot be avoided absolves the narrator from the full weight of his choice and tips the balance towards greater risk taking. The final gnome deciding the issue is that a brave man can escape from many a tight place.

---

[8] For a recent analysis of I see T. M. Charles-Edwards, *Wales and the Britons 350–1064* (Oxford, 2013), pp. 668–74.

Canu Heledd (III) on the whole has very different themes. The choices made by warriors are not directly relevant to the female narrator, although there is denunciation of those who failed to behave heroically, no doubt linked to events in the background tale. In one perplexing dialogue (98–101) Heledd criticizes bitterly a brother who was either cowardly or genuinely ill. In this poem we could have Heledd behaving like Llywarch as a non-combatant who goads unfairly, but it does not seem to have been a major factor in the loss of her brothers and Powys. She laments her woeful fate and specifically that her tongue caused it. Despite the similarities to Llywarch's statements it may not be due to similar behaviour, but in the absence of more narrative information it is impossible to be certain. One attested type of tale in which a woman could play an important role was as a bride given in marriage to assure peace between warring parties, in Old English a peace-weaver. I have suggested Heledd, like Branwen in the second branch of the *Mabinogi*, failed to cement peace, perhaps in Heledd's case by unwise speech, and that she, like Branwen, blamed herself for the resulting carnage. The choice of Heledd as narrator probably depended on her already having played a part in the story of Cynddylan; it is unlikely that she was an obscure or new character chosen by the poet to comment on the events.

It is probably necessary to postulate a pre-existing narrative about Heledd and the downfall of Cynddylan to explain the choice of a female narrator. Women are scarcely alluded to in the rest of the corpus. Much of Canu Heledd consists of laments, but the other cycles show men, like Llywarch, can perform this function. Several clues in the poetry suggest Heledd has taken over the mantle of the old Celtic goddess of sovereignty, mourning the loss of the rightful ruler of the land with no hope of a successor, and her own grief and changed circumstances.[9] In stanza 76 Heledd states that the land of Gyrthmwl if it were a woman would be weak and loudly wailing, just as she has presented herself. We see her wandering the devastated land of Powys in a hard goat-skin, contrasted to a splendid past when mead, a drink associated with sovereignty, of the region of Tren made her drunk. The names of her sisters seem to offer further clues to mythic associations with the land.[10] Heledd as Cynddylan's sister cannot have been the spouse of the king, so if her links with the sovereignty myth are correct it is another clue that the poet was working within the framework of an existing tale or set of traditions about her.

Ifor Williams also noted that the laments of Heledd allowed the poet to lament the borderland of his own day which had suffered from near constant warfare. A striking feature of the poetry is its scope despite the lack of narrative development. The cycle starts at the apex focussing on the ruler, Cynddylan, and moves on to

---

[9] There is a longer discussion in EWSP, pp. 140–49, with references to other examples of sovereignty figures in Irish and Welsh.
[10] These are discussed in the notes.

celebrate the members of his household troop and court in 'Stafell Gynddylan'. Eventually Heledd's wanderings in the ruined land lead to consideration of far more levels of society than is normal in medieval literature, celebrating the deeds of tillers of the soil and the lost normality of farming and herding. This is loss without hope of restitution, underlying the helplessness of female narrator. The reference to Llan Hyledd in the stanzas of the graves may suggest Heledd eventually sought refuge in the church, but there is no glimpse of peace for Heledd in the surviving verse.

Nature Imagery, Gnomes, and Proverbs

Most of the saga poems make use of nature imagery, gnomes, and proverbs, with the texts here no exception. While these elements may be used mechanically to fill out a stanza in some genres, they are generally integral to the artistry and effect of the saga poems. Nature description can provide a realistic background, as in some of the descriptions of the devastated land of Powys in III. The depiction of a wintry landscape in IV is both descriptive and directly relevant to the question of the wisdom of undertaking a dangerous and difficult expedition. Nature can also evoke a mood, with some of the frozen stasis of winter in IV conveyed to the audience. The brief evocation of the sea waves in the *marwnad* for Gwên is probably there for its sorrowful connotations, while the night time calls of the birds of prey in III.34–44 intensifies the effect of grief and helplessness of Heledd. Llywarch's lament in old age moves through the seasons in II.4–7 not to depict the realistic passage of time, but to show his character out of sympathy with each season. Nature imagery can also be metaphoric: Cynddylan as a single tree III.2, 16), the solid-looking bank which crumbles under pressure (I.9), the brevity of the life of a leaf (II.14). It is well worth puzzling out the reasons for and impact of nature descriptions, brief or sustained, in the poems.

Gnomes and proverbs are also a consistent element in the saga verse. Quite possibly this type of wisdom was both coined by and preserved by poets as part of their mystique since many of the medieval proverb lists draw on extant poems and others appear to be from lost *englynion*. Such wisdom was certainly highly valued, and gnomic poems are a recognized genre in Medieval Welsh bardic verse, with many overlaps with the saga tradition.[11] Generally speaking gnomes comment on what is usual or normative, often in a baldly factual way, and are divided by commentators into human and nature gnomes. (Obviously with the latter there can be an overlap between nature description and more general gnomic statements — sometimes the distinction is moot.) Human gnomes concern behaviour and society. Proverbs may be more metaphorical as in III.16c

[11] Nicolas Jacobs, *Early Welsh Gnomic and Nature Poetry*, pp. xvii–xxx.

ny elwir coet o vn prenn which speaks both of trees and warriors. The sententious element is a way of linking the particular experience of the saga character to that of the audience, although it is not so dominant as to make these pieces overtly wisdom literature. Llywarch's misplaced desire for glory would be a lesson to medieval Welsh aristocratic society, with the gnomic '*Cwl eu dyuot clot trameint*' both summarizing pithily the result of his goading and suggesting wider social recognition of the societal norms and truths which Llywarch violated. In the dialogue with Gwên Llywarch also uses both gnomes and nature imagery to obliquely challenge Gwên rather than directly accusing him. This is echoed by Heledd in her criticism of imperfect warriors beginning '*Ny mat*'. Heledd also draws back from the extremes of her personal grief with more generalized statements about the human condition which allows the audience to identify with her emotions, if not her specific plight. The debate in IV is carried out both in nature description and proverbs rather than specific analysis and thus offers a normative pattern for the warrior in assessing risk and gain.

Metrics

While study of the metrics of the saga *englynion* may seem a needless chore for those wishing to translate the texts, a good understanding of the structure of poems often requires metrical analysis, and appreciation of the poetry is enhanced in general. (Metrics is also important in many cases for assessing the reliability of a reading or proposed emendation.) A brief guide to the required features of the main types of early *englynion* will be given here, as well as various additional but optional ornaments. Particular attention should be paid to the way in which stanzas are linked in the poems since lyric works in Welsh rely more on metrical linking than development of themes or thought. Poems which are tightly structured metrically may appear rambling or needlessly repetitive in translation.

The *englyn* is the only stanzaic metre in early Welsh poetry, but various types are found. Originally the *englyn* had three lines as in the verse preserved in the Cambridge Juvencus manuscript; sometime before 1100 four-line types appeared and eventually replaced the earlier types in the works of the court poets.[12] However, two of the three-line types, the *englyn milwr* and the *englyn penfyr*, retained sufficient prestige or currency to be included in the list of twenty-four official bardic measures in the fourteenth century poetic treatise, *Gramadegau'r Penceirddiaid*. A third type found in the saga poetry is the *englyn byr crwca*, a term coined by John Morris Jones on the basis of its similarity to the four-line *englyn crwca*.

[12] See below on the dating implications of these texts; also Nerys Ann Jones, 'Y Gogynfeirdd a'r Englyn' in *Beirdd a Thywysogion: Barddoniaeth Llys yng Nghymru, Iwerddon a'r Alban*, ed. Morfydd E. Owen and Brynley F. Roberts (Caerdydd, 1996), pp. 288–301; EWSP, pp. 330–32.

The *englyn milwr* is the simplest with the least variety in form, and often little or no additional ornament. It consists of 3 lines of 7 syllables each,[13] with some lines a syllable longer or, more rarely, a syllable shorter. End rhyme appears to be obligatory in all three lines. Exs. I.5, II.7.

The *englyn penfyr* is much more varied. The version which most resembles the bardic 4-line standard, the *englyn unodl union*, is not fixed or standard in the 3-line form.[14] In the *englyn penfyr* the first line is lengthened and the second shortened. The end rhyme with the final two lines of the *englyn* can be found two to three syllables before the end of line a, at the point later called the *gwant*, but end rhyme may be dispensed with altogether in this opening line (unlike in the classic *englyn unodl union*). An internal rhyme in line a with the *gwant* is common, although considered a fault later. The remaining syllables of the lengthened first line form what is later called the *gair cyrch*, connected by metrical ornament to the following line. In the three-line version sometimes the link is with the first part of the opening line, and in many stanzas the *gair cyrch* has no formal connection. (This is almost invariably the case with the very common *heno, hediw, neithiwyr* as *gair cyrch* in saga poems.) Very often the *penfyr* stanzas display more non-obligatory ornamentation compared to the *milwr*, the longer and more complicated patterns offering more scope for elaboration.

> Exs. rhyming *gwant*, *gair cyrch* connected to line b by alliteration II.14
> rhyming *gwant*, *gair cyrch* connected to line a by rhyme II.1
> internal rhyme with the *gwant* I.2, I.28–29
> internal rhyme with the *gwant*; *gwant* does not rhyme with end rhyme I.6
> no rhyme on the *gwant*, *gair cyrch* connected to b I.12
> no rhyme on the *gwant*, *gair cyrch* unconnected I.1, III.18

The *englyn byr crwca* is comparatively uncommon (about 10% of the total) and as with the *englyn penfyr* there is variety of forms. In this type of stanza it is the second line which is lengthened, and the third shortened. Some resemble the classical form of the *englyn penfyr* with end rhyme before the extra syllables; others like many early *englynion penfyr* dispense with end rhyme here. The extra syllables operate like the *gair cyrch*, and as with the *englyn penfyr* there is not always a link. The rare type with two rhyming sections in b has no equivalent in the *englyn penfyr*.

---

[13] The forms are discussed in terms of syllable count which gives reasonable consistency. In recent scholarship stress count has dominated analysis of medieval Welsh metres of the *awdl* type. For a review of Welsh metrical scholarship see Marged Haycock, *Legendary Poems from the Book of Taliesin* (Aberystwyth, 2007), pp. 37–39. For a more detailed description of the forms and ornaments see EWSP, pp. 305–55.

[14] Nerys Ann Jones, 'Y Gogynfeirdd a'r Englyn', notes the various forms in works of the Poets of the Princes, including those which resemble the earlier 3-line types, pp. 290–94.

Exs. end rhyme in all three lines, with the extra syllables connected to the following line by rhyme II.9, III.96
end rhyme in all three lines but no link from b to c III.94
no end rhyme in b and no link to c III.54–56
no end rhyme in b but *gair cyrch* link to c and internal rhyme in b IV.
no end rhyme in b or link to c but b has 2 rhyming sections III.87, III.92

Early *englynion* poems tend to mix types while poems which appear to be later, and works by the Poets of the Princes tend to have predominately a single type.[15] There is a higher proportion of *penfyr* verses in Canu Heledd. The first verse in Canu Heledd is a four-line *englyn unodl union*, although the *gwant* does not rhyme with the end rhyme as would be normal in later bardic practice. The number of stanzas in poems is very variable. Single stanza poems or very brief poems are more common in antiquarian type verse, and are found in the later parts of Canu Heledd.

Besides the features of ornament which define the types of verses, there is a good deal of additional ornament which is optional. A major feature as can be seen in the discussion of basic metrical forms is rhyme, also used for additional ornament. Rhyme is between final syllables only. (Occasional two syllable rhymes can result accidentally from disyllabic verbal endings, etc.). Besides full rhyme matching both vowel or diphthong with the same consonant, there is generic rhyme where the vowel or diphthong is identical but the consonants can vary according to classes, such as all nasals with each other or /-d,-g/ and /-l, -r, -δ]/. Generic rhyme, also called *odl Wyddelig* or Irish rhyme, was once thought to be indicative of early date but late examples can be found. A rarer form of rhyme is *proest* which is a mirror image of generic rhyme: the consonants are identical but the vowel or diphthongs vary according to classes. The later four line *englyn proest* uses *proest* instead of the usual end rhyme, varying the vocalic element in each line. This latter feature is not attested in the earlier three-line versions.

Besides end rhyme, all these types of rhyme can be used internally in the line, or across lines in the linking of the *gair cyrch*. The same end rhyme is rarely found within the stanzas of a poem and where found it is usually in consecutive stanzas. It may be used intentionally to link stanzas (*cymeriad*); *cf.* II. 15, II.16. An additional type of rhyme found internally is *llusg*, rhyming of a final syllable with an internal syllable later in the line; ex. II.14c *Hi hen*; *eleni y ganet*, III.52b *ysef y hefras*. This is not common.

Alliteration is clearly a poetic ornament, but since it is not obligatory it is difficult to define the rules with precision. It can involve initial consonants only

---

[15] This is overwhelmingly the *englyn unodl union*, *Ibid.*, pp. 290–91. In the later looking three-line *englynion*, on the other hand, the *englyn milwr* is predominant.

(III.39c a'e llawch llwydit), consonant clusters and initial with consonant clusters (I.10c brwyt briw, II.4a *b*aglann brenn, IV.45c cledyr kat callon), and sometimes there is consonance — that is internal consonants forming part of the pattern (I.28c glew galwytheint, IV.14b crin calaw caled). Rhyme, alliteration and consonance can be used together in more elaborate patterns (II.16c heneint heint a hoet, III.25c dygystud deurud dagreu, IV.16b glas glan guilan). Where a line has a clear caesura it is normal to find alliteration, internal rhyme or both across the divide (II.7b neut rud rych; neut crych egin, I.21a tonn tyruit; toit eruit, II.6b rud cogeu; goleu ynghwyn). Sometimes alliteration in this position has a mirror pattern: IV.1b llicrid rid; reuihid llin.

Mutated consonants appear to alliterate with radicals in early poetry (III.44b ar waet gwyr gwelit, I.6b pan wisc glew y'r ystre, I.10 am glawd caer, II.16a vym pedwar prifgas III. vn prenn ygwydvit a gouit arnaw, IV.27a ni'm guna pryder im Pridein, IV.2a ton tra thon toid tu tir). This is not necessarily an archaism based on poetic patterns from the period prior to full development of initial mutations, but probably based on the underlying perception of the word as it exists in its non-mutated form. The sounds produced by radical and mutations of the radical may also have been thought to be sufficiently similar to alliterate. By the time of strict *cynghanedd* it is clear that actual sounds were matched, i.e. an initial /g/ from /k/ would alliterate a word beginning with /g/ rather than with a word beginning with /k/. When alliteration between the radical and its mutated version ceased is unclear, and it may have co-existed with alliteration between actual sounds from different radicals.[16] Some lines would appear to alliterate in this way (I.15c ar glawd gorlas, II.7c etlit y'm edrych y'th yluin, II.15a a gereis i yr yn was yssy gas gennyf). /H/ often appears to alliterate with itself, but may also alliterate with vowels which alliterate with each other (II.16c heneint heint a hoet, II.14c, III.80c hir hwyl heul; hwy vyghouyon, II.17a wyf hen, wyf unic, wyf annelwic oer, III.52b ysef y hefras eiryoet, III.38a Eryr Eli echeidw myr, I.3a neut atwen ar vy awen/ yn hanuot o un achen).

For the stanzaic *englynion* poems perhaps the most important non-obligatory metrical feature is *cymeriad* in all its forms. *Cymeriad* refers to the linking of metrical units, in the *englynion* most usually of stanzas. Most of the above ornaments can be used in this way. Rhyme and alliteration can be found from the end of the dialogue between Gwên and Llywarch and the opening of the *marwnad* (I.14, I.15). In II the final word of stanza 15, *kyuadas*, rhymes internally with *prifgas* in 16a. Alliteration links the end II.16 to the beginning of II.17. The final stanzas of II, 17–20, are linked in a chain by verbal repetition. *Wyf tridyblic* at the end of 17 is linked to 18a *Wyf tridyblic hen*. The end of 18 and the beginning of 19 are linked by the repetition of *ny'm kar*. Stanzas 19 and 20 similarly have *na'm dygret/ ny'm dygret*. The sequence ends with *wyf hen* bringing it back round to the beginning of

[16] Discussed in EWSP, pp. 338–43.

17, a framing device.[17] This is common for sequences linked by chain *cymeriad*, but is also often found over a complete poem or to mark out a discrete section; cf. the *marwnad* proper to Gwên which begins and ends with his name (I.15-23).

The most striking type of *cymeriad* in the saga *englynion* is verbal repetition, the repetition or close echoing of opening words linking several stanzas (*cymeriad geiriol*). In poem II before the closing chain *cymeriad* there are 3 stanzas beginning *Kynn bum kein-vaglawc* followed by 7 stanzas beginning with *Baglan brenn*, the first four of which are also linked in the following lines by description of four seasons in Llywarch's life. Stanzas 11 and 12 have verbal repetition in all three lines, a pattern also called incremental repetition. The first two poems in Canu Heledd not only have extensive *cymeriad geiriol* in the opening line, but repetition of other verbal patterns in lines b and c. Except in dialogues where the regular interchange between speakers provides its own structure, *cymeriad* is an extremely important device in shaping the poem.

Manuscripts, Authorship, Dating, Language

The earliest manuscripts of the texts in this volume are from a considerably later period than their presumed date of composition. The Black Book of Carmarthen dates to the mid-thirteenth century, the White Book of Rhydderch from the mid-fourteenth century, and the Red Book of Hergest from the late-fourteenth century.[18] In addition some readings are taken from post-medieval manuscripts such as John Davies Mallwyd's NLW 4973B, and the late copies of portions of the White Book now missing. This is a wealth of manuscripts for the Red Book/White Book texts in Welsh terms, and it is clear they do not come from an immediate common exemplar.[19] The evidence from errors, omissions, traces of older orthography, etc., suggests that lost written exemplars may go back to an earlier period. The inclusion of two *englynion* poems written in an early-tenth century hand in the margin of the Cambridge Juvencus manuscript provides invaluable evidence that verse similar to the saga poems linguistically, stylistically and metrically was composed in the Old Welsh period. However, it is unclear whether or not this marginalia points to the existence of written poetic manuscripts at this date.[20] The impression in general is that the texts are in

---

[17] This becomes the most used *cymeriad* in the works of the Poets of Princes, Nerys Ann Jones, 'Y Gogynfeirdd a'r Englyn', p. 290, sometimes combined with *cymeriad geiriol*.

[18] See Daniel Huws, *Medieval Welsh Manuscripts* (Cardiff, 2000) on the dating and provenance of the medieval manuscripts.

[19] Jenny Rowland, 'The Manuscript Tradition of the Red Book *Englynion*', SC 18/19 (1983-1984), pp. 79-95.

[20] For the dating see Helen McKee, 'Scribes and Glosses from Dark Age Wales: The Cambridge Juvencus Manuscript', CMCS 39 (2000), pp. 1-22. Both poems are edited by Ifor Williams in BBCS VI (1933), 'Tri Englyn y Juvencus', pp. 101-10 and 'Naw Englyn y Juvencus', pp. 205-24, combined and translated into English by Rachel Bromwich as 'The Juvencus Poems' in *The Beginnings of Welsh Poetry*, ed. R. Bromwich (Cardiff, 1972), pp. 89-12. There is also an edition and discussion of the 9 by Marged Haycock, *Blodeugerdd Barddas o Ganu Crefyddol Cynnar* (Llandybïe,1994), pp. 3-29.

relatively good order, with little evidence of long oral transmission. The scribes habitually modernized the texts they copied, so only the occasional error or archaism may suggest written exemplars from an earlier period.

Welsh scholars have long emphasized the role of the Welsh bard as a praise poet, leading to some unease about the authorship of other attested genres of early Welsh poetry. Outside of praise poetry credible attributions to named poets are not found in the early period, particularly since many genres, like the saga *englynion*, rely on the use of persona. Most Welsh scholars have accepted that the saga *englynion* were the work of the highest poets, the bards, if not their primary and most prestigious poetry. However, some critics have argued that the *englynion* are the works of lower status bards, or even non-bardic popular poets.[21] The medieval manuscripts consistently segregate *englynion* and *awdlau*, encouraging this conclusion, even though it may be solely classification on metrical grounds. The Poets of the Princes, certainly at the pinnacle of the bardic order, composed in both metres, for the same patrons. There is no clear evidence for differences in style, language or contents in these works in the two measures.[22] Apart from praise poetry, *englynion* and *awdlau* are used for most poetic genres, although there are some genres where one type predominates. Allowing for differences of content and date of composition, the saga *englynion* display bardic learning, language and metrical skill similar to that of the Poets of the Princes. They were treasured long enough to be preserved in writing in the great medieval compilations of Welsh verse. All evidence points to the saga *englynion* as being bardic poetry with the caveat that we actually know very little about any gradations in status of the poets.

Early Welsh poetry is notoriously difficult to date. In recent years there has been substantial revision of some previously-accepted dating. This revisionism has not been applied to the saga *englynion* in any major way so far, but the re-examination of the language of *The Gododdin*, the poems of the Book of Taliesin, and the Poets of the Princes is bound to be helpful in dating, if only by shaking up previous certainties. Many linguistic forms, orthographic features and metrical practices once thought early may not be as diagnostic as previously believed.[23] The composition of saga *englynion* undoubtedly spans a long time period; with the exception of a few probably inserted verses the poems in this volume would appear to lie towards the beginning, before c. 1000.[24]

---

[21] Discussed in EWSP, pp. 335–63.
[22] See Nerys Ann Jones, 'Y Gogynfeirdd a'r Englyn', pp. 294–98. On the lack of *englynion* in the Book of Taliesin, see Haycock, *Legendary Poems*, pp. 8–9.
[23] For a discussion of some of the relevant forms thought to be diagnostic and reference to ongoing studies, see Haycock, *Legendary Poems*, pp. 21–25, and Jacobs, *Early Welsh Gnomic and Nature Poetry*, pp. xli–xlv and the detailed study of verbal forms by Simon Rodway, *Dating Medieval Welsh Literature: Evidence from the Verbal System* (Aberystwyth, 2013).
[24] Jacobs favours later dating, *Early Welsh Gnomic and Nature Poetry*, p. xliv.

The language of these pieces has been modernized by scribes to normative Middle Welsh. Poetry may have been more resistant to wholesale modernization than prose, but only forms which would affect the metre and some errors in modernization can be diagnostic as either early or late. For instance the last verse of the nine Juvencus *englynion* can easily be rewritten as standard Middle Welsh, with only the earlier form of the verbal noun ending *–if*, in Middle Welsh *–i*, providing evidence for an early date.[25] If our hypothetical Middle Welsh scribe had modernized *molim* as *moli* this evidence would have been lost, although the possibility of restoring internal rhyme would have strongly suggested an earlier form lay behind the more modern.[26] Conversely a verbal noun ending in *–i* rhyming with *–i* would suggest a later date for composition, as would other non-orthographic changes from Old Welsh which would affect metre.[27] It is rare to get a clear indication of an exclusively Old Welsh form. It is also generally impossible to be sure when a form became obsolete in the conservative language of the poets, or whether older forms co-existed for a period with newer ones, analogous to the poetic uses of variant verbal forms. Obviously late forms are therefore more diagnostic, but not definitive. These are rare in the saga *englynion* and in some instances occur in stanzas which may have been added or modified. Syntax also may offer clues to language change, and therefore dating. Again later features may be more significant for dating, such as the occasional use of the absolute ending in a non-simplex verb, the positioning of infixed pronouns, and use of the periphrastic construction with *mae*. On the other hand, the predominate syntax of the copula, the expression of possession and treatment of clauses may be early. Loan words from English are very rare, excluding even those attested in the works of the Poets of the Princes. The notes to the texts indicate possible early or late features and whether they appear in places which make them significant for dating.

Metrical features may also be used to provide a rough chronology. As noted above, the *englynion* in the margin of the Juvencus manuscript, no later than the early tenth century, are comparable to the earlier saga *englynion*. From the end of the Old Welsh period there is a four-line *englyn* in a late eleventh-century manuscript.[28] Four-lined *englynion* are employed exclusively in the works attributed to named Poets of the Princes. The *englyn proest* is the true four-line replacement for the *englyn milwr*, but this use of *proest* in all lines for rhyme is

---

[25] *Un a ued a phwyll a pheir/ Uch nef, is nef yn gyweir/ Nyd gorgnif molif map meir*. Original: *un hamed hapuil haper/uuc nem isnem intcouer/ nitguorgnim molim map meir* (Ifor Williams, *The Beginnings of Welsh Poetry*, p. 102).

[26] In fact, the poem in the Llywarch cycle to Maen has a very similar reading. All the mss. have *nyt ouer gnif ym hogi maen*; the correction to *hogif* is nearly certain. See EWSP, p. 411.

[27] See for instance the discussion of rhymes in III.52 and III.53 and syllabic length in II.1–3.

[28] See Paul Russell, 'The *englyn* to St Padarn Revisited', CMCS 63 (2012), pp. 1–14 and Haycock, *Blodeugerdd*, pp. 242–43. This is an *englyn gwastad*, the more natural expansion of the *englyn milwr* which is rarely attested in the works of the Poets of the Princes.

not attested in the earlier poetry. The *englyn unodl union* is closer to the *englyn penfyr*, although there is far greater standardization of rhyme at the *gwant* and linking of the *gair cyrch*.²⁹ If we accept that the saga verse was written by the professional poets, metrical features would suggest the main body of saga poetry predates their poetry. However, the fact that two of the three-lined types were named in the list of twenty-four 'official' bardic metres in the fourteenth century and the evident later date of some poems may suggest that different practices prevailed for the mainly anonymous non-praise poetry genres.³⁰ Nevertheless, apart from genre the saga *englynion* resemble recognized bardic verse and are more sophisticated metrically than most of the three-lined poems with clear late features. In my view it is easier to plot a development from the metrics of saga verse to the codification of the four-line metres at the highest bardic levels, while granting that in certain genres the simpler forms continued to be used in a far less skilled manner than their earlier models.

There is evidence as well that the saga poems were already treasured as *hengerdd* by the Poets of the Princes, and imitated by them in their compositions.³¹ This goes a long way to confirming their high bardic status and is also suggestive of an earlier date. While it would be desirable to have more certainty about authorship and dating, the reception of the saga *englynion* in the Middle Ages and beyond is not in doubt. This is poetry which was preserved by the poets orally and in writing, and long treasured. The genre is one which would be of interest and acceptable in every part of Wales, unlike praise poetry to a specific regional patron. The stories encompass the fabled and always interesting Old North and many areas of Wales, dealt with the dilemmas and emotions of everyday aristocratic life, and their style was adaptable to other genres such as dramatized religious lyrics and antiquarian verse. Some of the poems, or individual stanzas, are undoubtedly later, attesting to continuing popularity and interest. Lack of secure dating and context is not a barrier to appreciating this verse to this day.

On the Edition

It is to be hoped that this edition could be used by anyone with a knowledge of Middle Welsh. It is not intended to be a full scholarly edition. Unlike many other medieval Welsh texts there is an English edition which is relatively recent. I have therefore chosen to present a text suitable for classroom or private study, using

---

[29] See Nerys Ann Jones, 'Y Gogynfeirdd a'r Englyn', pp. 290–94. Poems with a true mixture of types are also rare in the later poems as compared to the saga *englynion*.
[30] Jacobs, *Early Welsh Gnomic and Nature Poetry*, pp. xxxix–xlv. Alternatively, respect for the *hengerdd* in *englynion* may have preserved status for a metre no longer used by the highest poets.
[31] Nerys Ann Jones, 'Hengerdd in the Age of the Poets of the Princes', in *Beyond Gododdin: Dark Age Scotland in Medieval Wales*, ed. Alex Woolf (St. Andrews, 2013), pp. 49, 54–56, 71–74.

approaches gained from my experience of teaching *hengerdd*. I have found many students initially find it difficult or unrewarding to wade through long, involved notes which can more often than not lead to an inconclusive result. The notes are therefore not so much simplified as streamlined, and anyone seeking greater detail can look in *Early Welsh Saga Poetry* and other referenced works. (Where additional work has been done since *Early Welsh Saga Poetry* was published I have included more detail or provided references.) Occasionally the process of proposing an emendation or interpretation of language and syntax is covered more fully for several reasons: it may be important for interpretation to know how reliable the proposed solution may be, it can act as a model for those students who want to explore the editorial process more fully, and it provides reference to more recently published textual notes. Some notes may conversely seem overly elementary, but reflect representative student difficulties over the years.

Like *Early Welsh Saga Poetry* this edition is heavily dependent on *Canu Llywarch Hen*, and a wealth of Medieval Welsh scholarship. Of particular importance in the intervening period has been the publication of the edition of the works of the Poets of the Princes (*Cyfres Beirdd y Tywysogion*), the reassessment of Welsh bardic poetry arising from that, and the edition of the poems in the Book of Taliesin ascribed to the legendary figure. As noted in the section on dating there has also been a considerable amount of work on linguistic change and orthography. *Geiriadur Prifysgol Cymru* (GPC) is complete and searchable data bases have been produced. Inevitably this has led to some changes in interpretation, and will undoubtedly lead to more in the future.

This edition can be used on its own, but more meaningful experience can be gained by following up references, and using the dictionary and grammar. A translation and explanation of a form can be found in the glossary or notes, but examination of its context in GPC or *A Grammar of Middle Welsh* will give a better overview of Middle Welsh.[32] It is more than helpful to have a knowledge of grammatical terms, and to aid acquaintance with the terminology I have avoided abbreviations of grammatical terms except for the most common. Prose texts can give a false sense of understanding the language which poetry quickly corrects! Even though the style of the *englynion* is not overly artificial, the poetry is concise and requires careful consideration of how every word relates to the others. The glossary will provide a minimal translation, but in many cases the notes should also be consulted. Interpretive notes are also included. There is repetition in the notes because readers of poetry unlike those of prose texts may dip in rather than start from the beginning, and some points are better learned

---

[32] A further challenge for the reader would be to note mutations which are not shown in the medieval orthography and to understand the reasons for mutations, indicated and not. As explained above it is also rewarding and illuminating to examine the metrics.

by seeing several examples. The Bibliography is mainly for follow up reading, plus references to works cited in the notes.

Verses are indicated in the manuscripts, but the poetry is not laid out in lines. In order to encourage metrical analysis I have not used a line layout which immediately flags the differences in *englynion* types. Light punctuation, not necessarily that of the manuscripts, has been added although occasionally this favours one interpretation over another. Capitalization is also editorial. While some titles are found in the manuscripts, there are very few in the texts included in this volume. II, which is first in the manuscripts, is called 'Englynion Llywarch' in versions apart from that of the Red Book, but this is probably intended to cover all of the *englynion* which follow. The editorial titles generally follow those used in *Canu Llywarch Hen*. The notes offer suggestions as to probable misordering of stanzas and intrusive stanzas, but no changes in order have been made in the texts other than the inclusion of the opening stanza in I.

The text here has been emended for simpler reading; full manuscript variants can be found in EWSP. For I–III readings have been taken from more than one manuscript, although the Red Book of Hergest is generally followed. The text of IV is from the sole manuscript, the Black Book of Carmarthen. The incorporation of better readings in I–III taken from the later copies of the White Book and NLW 4973B are noted. Obvious and long-accepted emendations from *Canu Llywarch Hen* are also used, with the manuscript reading in the notes. Square brackets indicate an emendation which goes beyond variant readings, < > indicates text in the manuscript which should be omitted. Where an emendation is uncertain it has not been included in the text, but possibilities for variant readings are explored in the notes.

A Note on Emendation

The first responsibility of an editor should be to try to understand the text as it has come down to us, and texts of this date are bound to throw up some intractable problems of translation. However, sometimes the text appears to be clearly defective. A line may appear to be ungrammatical or make no sense. A reading may look considerably later than the supposed date of the poem. Metrical irregularities may also indicate the text is problematic. The need for emendation may be obvious or more subjective. It should not be done lightly to 'improve' the text in the eye of the editor or to justify a specific dating or interpretation. Emendation normally should be based on an understanding of how the text may have become corrupted. If text were altered or lost during oral transmission it may be impossible to speculate, but many copying errors are specific enough to justify restoring a better reading. Ideally then some sort of mechanism for explaining the error should be proposed even though human error can sometimes be totally random.

Anyone copying a text will be aware of errors which can creep in. In IV.5a 'Llym Awel' the scribe wrote 'eiry' twice, but underdotted the first to indicate it should be excluded. In 12a the 'v' was omitted in 'Gvenin' but inserted above. In 7b, however, the scribe did not catch the omission of 'v' in 'gint', clearly an error for 'gvint'. Miscopying may involve looking forward or backwards to other words or letters in the exemplar. The scribe may not have understood a reading, and sought to substitute a more comprehensible word. Marginal entries might have been copied into the original text. Where the exemplar had gaps or was too difficult to read no attempt at reconstruction could be made.

Since Welsh scribes generally undertook to reproduce texts in their own orthographic system many emendations depend on understanding the systems the scribe may have been copying from and how errors could arise from errors in modernizing. For instance in I.2b 'llem awel' it is argued that the scribe failed to change the e of his exemplar to y since *llem* could have been the feminine form of the adjective before *awel*. A t in a system like that of IV could be misinterpreted by a scribe not totally familiar with the orthography; cf. I.15b. Old Welsh orthography may lie behind other errors. Some letter forms could be mistaken for another in various periods, such as c and t or r and n.

A number of emendations depend on the errors which could arise in the reading of minims. The term refers to the identical strokes which formed the letters i, n, u or v, and m, making *minimum* the poster word for medieval scribal unreadability. Taking into account the various periods and schools of Welsh orthography and confusion of insular r and n minims can also lie behind words with r, w, e, and y as well as i, n, u, v and m. It was easy to write too few or too many strokes, and also to omit a suspension mark over i to indicate 'in', or misread an h with a short ascender. A proposed emendation might have to follow an original through more than one hypothetical copy with different orthographic errors.

Also useful in interpretation and emendation is comparison with bardic usage and vocabulary in other medieval Welsh verse. There are many collocations of words which can support an emendation. Direct echoes of the saga verse may be found in other poems, and in the proverb lists. Beyond the usefulness in establishing the text, such echoes help to confirm the place of the saga *englynion* within the bardic tradition.

TEXTS

I

'Gwên a Llywarch'

1. Teneu fy ysgwyd ar asswy fy nhu.
   Cybwyf hen, as gallaf
   Ar rodwydd orlas gwiliaf.

2. Na wisc wedy kwyn. Na vit vrwyn dy vryt.
   Llem awel; chwerw gwenwyn.
   Amgyhud vy mam mab yt wyf.

3. Neut atwen ar vy awen
   Yn hanuot o un achen.
   Trigwyd oric elwic, a Wen.

4. Llym vym par, llachar ygryt.
   Armaaf y wylyaw ryt.
   Kynnyt anghwyf, Duw gennyt.

5. O diegyd a'th welif.
   O'th ry ledir a'th gwynif.
   Na choll wyneb gwr ar gnif.

6. Ny chollaf dy wyneb, trinwosep wr,
   Pan wisc glew y'r ystre.
   Porthaf gnif kynn mudif lle.

7. Redegawc tonn ar hyt traeth.
   Ech adaf torrit aruaeth.
   Kat agdo — gnawt ffo ar ffraeth.

8. Yssit ym a lauarwyf.
   Briwaw pelydyr parth y bwyf.
   Ny lauaraf na ffowyf.

9. Medal migned; kalet riw.
   Rac carn cann tal glann a vriw.
   Edewit ny wnelher ny diw.

10. Gwasgarawt neint am glawd caer.
    A minneu armaaf
    Ysgwyt brwyt briw kynn techaf.

11. Y corn a'th rodes di Vryen
    A'e arwest eur am y en —
    Chwyth yndaw o'th daw aghen.

12. Yr ergryt aghen rac angwyr Lloegyr
    Ny lygraf vym mawred.
    Ny duhunaf rianed.

13. Tra vum i yn oet y gwas draw
    A wisc o eur y ottoew
    Bydei re ruthrwn y waew.

14. Diheu diweir dy waes:
    Ti yn vyw a'th dyst ry las.
    Ny bu eidyl hen yn was.

'Marwnad Gwên'

15. Gwen wrth Lawen yd welas neithwyr.
    [Yr] athuc ny techas.
    Oer adrawd ar glawd gorlas.

16. Gwen wrth Lawen yd wylwys neithwyr
    A'r ysgwyt ar y ysgwyd.
    Can bu mab ymi bu hywyd.

17. Gwen wrth Lawen yd wyliis neithwyr
    A'r ysgwyt ar y gnis.
    Kan bu mab ymi nyt egis.

18. Gwen gwgyd, gochawd vy mryt.
    Dy leas ys mawr …
    Casnar. Nyt car a'th ladawr.

19. Gwen vordwyt tylluras a wylyas neithwyr
    Ygoror ryt orlas.
    A chan bu mab ymi ny thechas.

20. Gwen, gwydwn dy eissillut.
    Ruthyr eryr yn ebyr oedut.
    Betwn dedwyd dianghut.

21. Tonn tyruit, toit eruit.
    Pan ant kynrein ygovit,
    Gwen, gwae ryhen o'th etlit.

22. Tonn tyruit, toit aches.
    Pan ant kynrein y neges,
    Gwen, gwae ryhen ry'th golles.

23. Oed gwr vy mab; oed disgywen hawl,
    Ac oed nei y Vryen.
    Ar ryt orlas y llas Gwen.

24. Prennyal dywal, gal ysgwn,
    Goruc ar Lloegyr llu cyngrwn.
    Bed Gwen uab Llywarch Hen hwn.

25. Pedwar meib ar hugeint a'm bu,
    Eurdorchawc, tywyssawc llu.
    Oed Gwen goreu onadu.

26. Pedwar meib ar hugeint a'm bwyat,
    Eurdorchawc, tywyssawc cat.
    Oed Gwen goreu mab o'e dat.

27. Pedwar meib ar hugeint a'm bwyn,
    Eurdorchawc, twywssawc vnbynn.
    Y wrth Wen gweissyonein oedyn.

28. Pedwar meib ar hugeint yg kenueint Lywarch
    O wyr glew galwytheint.
    Cwl eu dyuot clot trameint.

29. Pedwar meib ar hugeint a ueithyeint vyg knawt —
    Drwy vyn tauawt llesseint.
    Da dyuot bychot. Colledeint.

II

'Cân yr Henwr'

1. Kynn bum kein-vaglawc bum kyffes-eiryawc.
   Keinmygyr uy eres.
   Gwyr Argoet eiryoet a'm porthes.

2. Kynn bum kein-uaglawc bum hy.
   A'm kynnwyssit yg kyuyrdy
   Powys, paradwys Gymry.

3. Kynn bum kein-vaglawc bum eiryan.
   Oed kynwaew vym par; oed kynwan.
   Wyf keuyngrwm, wyf trwm, wyf truan.

4. Baglan brenn, neut kynhayaf.
   Rud redyn; melyn kalaf.
   Neur digereis a garaf.

5. Baglan brenn, neut gayaf hynn.
   Yt uyd llauar gwyr ar llyn.
   Neut diannerch vy erchwyn.

6. Baglan brenn, neut gwaeannwyn.
   Rud cogeu; goleu ynghwyn.
   Wyf digarat gan uorwyn.

7. Baglan brenn, neut kynteuin.
   Neut rud rych; neut crych egin.
   Etlit ym edrych y'th yluin.

8. Baglan brenn, ganghen [n]odawc,
   Kynhelych hen hiraethawc,
   Llywarch lleueryd uodawc.

9. Baglan brenn, ganghen galet,
   A'm kynnwyss y Duw diffret. I'th elwir
   Prenn kywir kynniret.

10. Baglan brenn, byd ystywell.
    A'm kynhelych a uo gwell.
    Neut wyf Lywarch lauar pell.

11. Kymwed y mae heneint
    A mi o'm gwallt y'm deint,
    A'r cloyn a gerynt yr ieueinc.

12. Y mae heneint yn kymwed a mi
    O'm gwallt y'm danned,
    A'r cloyn a gerynt wraged.

13. Dyr gwenn gwynt; gwynn gne godre
    Gwyd; dewr hyd; diwlyd bre.
    Eidyl hen; hwyr y dyre.

14. Y deilen honn — neu's kenniret gwynt.
    Gwae hi o'e thynghet.
    Hi hen; eleni y ganet.

15. A gereis i yr yn was yssy gas gennyf:
    Merch estrawn a march glas.
    Neut nat mi eu kyuadas.

16. Vym pedwar prifgas eirmoet
    Yt gyueruydynt yn vn oet:
    Pas a heneint, heint a hoet.

17. Wyf hen, wyf unic, wyf annelwic oer,
    Gwedy gwely keinmic.
    Wyf truan, wyf tridyblic.

18. Wyf tridyblic hen, wyf annwadal drut,
    Wyf ehut, wyf annwar.
    Y sawl a'm karawd ny'm kar.

19. Ny'm kar rianed; ny'm kenniret neb.
    Ny allaf darymret.
    Wi a agheu na'm dygret.

20. Ny'm dygret na hun na hoen
    Gwedy lleas Llawr a Gwen.
    Wyf annwar abar — wyf hen.

21. Truan a dynghet a dynget y Lywarch
    Yr y nos y ganet:
    Hir gnif heb escor lludet.

III

Canu Heledd

'Prologue'

1. Sefwch allann, vorynnyon, a syllwch
   Gyndylan werydre.
   Llys Benngwern neut tande.
   Gwae ieueinc a eidun brotre.

'Marwnad Cynddylan'

2. Vn prenn ygwydvit a gouit arnaw —
   O dieinc ys odit.
   Ac a uynno Duw, derffit.

3. Kynndylan callon iaen gaeaf,
   A want twrch trwy y benn,
   Cu a rodeist yr cwrwf Trenn.

4. Kynndylan callon godeith wannwyn
   O gyflwyn anghyuyeith,
   Yn amwyn Tren, tref diffeith.

5. Kyndylan befyrbost kywlat,
   Kadwynawc, kildynnyawc cat,
   Amucsei Tren, tref y dat.

6. Kyndylan beuyrbwyll ovri,
   Kadwynawc, kynndynnyawc llu,
   Amucsei Tren hyt tra vu.

7. Kyndylan callon milgi,
   Pan disgynnei yg kymelri
   Cat calaned a ledi.

8. Kynndylan callon hebawc,
   Buteir ennwir gynndeiryawc,
   Keneu Kyndrwyn kyndynyawc.

9. Kyndylan callon gwythhwch,
   Pan disgynnei ym priffwch
   Cat kalaned yn deudrwch.

10. Kyndylan gulhwch gynnifiat llew,
    Bleid dilin disgynnyat.
    Nyt atuer twrch tref y dat.

11. Kyndylan hyt tra attat yd adei
    Y gallon mor wylat
    Gantaw mal y gwrwf y gat.

12. Kyndylan Powys, borffor wych yt.
    Kell esbyt, bywyt ior,
    Keneu Kyndrwyn kwynitor.

13. Kyndylan Wynn uab Kyndrwyn —
    Nyt mat wisc baraf am y drwyn
    Gwr ny bo gwell no morwyn.

14. Kyndylan, kymwyat wyt.
    Armeithyd na bydy[d] lwyt.
    Am Drebwll twll dy ysgwyt.

15. Kynndylan, kae di y riw
    Yn y daw Lloegyrwys hediw.
    Amgeled am vn ny diw.

16. Kyndylan, kae di y nenn
    Yn y daw Lloegyrwys drwy Dren.
    Ny elwir coet o vn prenn.

17. Gan vyg callon i mor dru
    Kysylltu y styllot du gwynngnawt
    Kyndylan, kyngran can llu.

'Stafell Gynddylan'

18. Stauell Gyndylan ys tywyll heno,
    Heb dan, heb wely.
    Wylaf wers; tawaf wedy.

19. Stauell Gyndylan ys tywyll heno,
    Heb dan, heb gannwyll.
    Namyn Duw, pwy a'm dyry pwyll?

20. Stauell Gyndylan ys tywyll heno,
    Heb dan, heb oleuat.
    Etlit a'm daw amdanat.

21. Stauell Gyndylan ys tywyll y nenn
    Gwedy gwen gyweithyd.
    Gwae ny wna da a'e dyuyd.

22. Stauell Gyndylan, neut athwyt heb wed.
    Mae ym bed dy yscwyt.
    Hyt tra uu, ny bu dollglwyt.

23. Stauell Gyndylan ys digarat heno
    Gwedy yr neb pieuat.
    O wi a angheu, byrr y'm gat?

24. Stauell Gyndylan nyt esmwyth heno
    Ar benn carrec hytwyth.
    Heb ner, heb niuer, heb amwyth.

25. Stauell Gyndylan ys tywyll heno,
    Heb dan, heb gerdeu.
    Dygystud deurud dagreu.

26. Stauell Gyndylan ys tywyll heno,
    Heb dan, heb deulu.
    Hidyl vyn deigyr men yt gynnu.

27. Stauell Gyndylan — a'm gwan y gwelet
    Heb doet, heb dan.
    Marw vy glyw; buw mu hunan.

28. Stauell Gyndylan ys peithiawc heno
    Gwedy ketwyr bodawc:
    Eluan, Kyndylan kaeawc.

29. Stauell Gyndylan ys oergrei heno
    Gwedy y parch a'm buei.
    Heb wyr, heb wraged a'e katwei.

30. Stauell Gyndylan ys araf heno
    Gwedy colli y hynaf.
    Y mawr drugarawc Duw, pa wnaf?

31. Stauell Gyndylan ys tywyll y nenn
    Gwedy dyua o Loegyrwys
    Kyndylan ac Eluan Powys.

32. Stauell Gyndylan ys tywyll heno
    O blant Kyndrwyn[yn]:
    Kynon a Gwiawn a Gwyn.

33. Stauell Gyndylan a'm erwan pob awr
    Gwedy mawr ymgyuyrdan
    A weleis ar dy benntan.

'Eryr Eli'

34. Eryr Eli — ban y lef heno.
    Llewssei gwyar llynn:
    Creu callon Kyndylan Wynn.

35. Eryr Eli gorelwi heno.
    Ygwaet gwyr gwynnovi.
    Ef ygoet; trwm hoet ymi.

36. Eryr Eli a glywaf heno.
    Creulyt yw; ny's beidyaf.
    Ef ygoet, trwm hoet arnaf.

37. Eryr Eli — gorthrymet heno
    Dyffrynt Meissir myget.
    Dir Brochuael, hir ry godet.

38. Eryr Eli — echeidw myr.
    Ny threid pyscawt yn ebyr.
    Gelwit, gwelit o waet gwyr.

39. Eryr Eli gorymda coet heno.
    Kyuor e kinyawa.
    A'e llawch — llwydit y draha.

'Eryr Pengwern'

40. Eryr Penngwern, penngarn llwyt — heno
    Aruchel y atleis.
    Eidic am gic a gereis.

41. Eryr Penngwern, penngarn llwyt — heno
    Aruchel y euan.
    Eidic am gic Kynndylan.

42. Eryr Penngwern, pengarn llwyt — heno
    Aruchel y adaf.
    Eidic am gic a garaf.

43. Eryr Penngwern — pell galwawt heno.
    Ar waet gwyr gwylawt.
    Ry gelwir Trenn tref difawt.

44. Eryr Penngwern — pell gelwit heno.
    Ar waet gwyr gwelit.
    Ry gelwir Trenn tref lethrit.

'Eglwysau Basa'

45. Eglwysseu Bassa y orffowys heno,
    Y diwed ymgynnwys,
    Cledyr kat, callon Argoetwis.

46. Eglwysseu Bassa ynt ffaeth heno.
    Vyn tauawt a'e gwnaeth.
    Rud ynt wy; rwy vy hiraeth.

47. Eglwysseu Bassa ynt yng heno
    Y etiued Kyndrwyn[yn]:
    Tir mablan Kyndylan Wynn.

48. Eglwysseu Bassa ynt tirion heno.
    Ys gwaedlyt eu meillyon.
    Rud ynt wy; rwy vyng callon.

49. Eglwysseu Bassa collassant eu breint
    Gwedy y diua o Loegyrwys
    Kyndylan ac Eluan Powys.

50. Eglwysseu Bassa ynt diua heno —
    Y chetwyr ny phara.
    Gwyr a wyr a mi yma.

51. Eglwysseu Bassa ynt varuar heno,
    A minneu wyf dyar.
    Rud ynt wy; rwy vyg galar.

'Y Drefwen'

52. Y Drefwenn ym bronn y coet —
    Ysef y hefras eiryoet:
    Ar wyneb y gwellt y gwaet.

53. Y Drefwenn yn y thymyr —
    Y hefras yglas vyuyr:
    Y gwaet a dan draet y gwyr.

54. Y Drefwenn yn y dyffrynt —
    Llawen y bydeir wrth gyuamrud kat.
    Y gwerin neur derynt.

55. Y Drefwenn rwng Trenn a Throdwyd —
    Oed gnodach ysgwyt tonn yn dyuot o gat
    Nogyt ych y echwyd.

56. Y Drefwenn rwng Trenn a Thraual —
    Oed gnodach y gwaet ar wyneb y gwellt
    Noc eredic brynar.

'Ffreuer'

57. Gwynn y byt, Freuer. Mor yw diheint heno
    Gwedy colli kenueint.
    O anffawt vyn tauawt yt lesseint.

58. Gwyn y byt, Freuer. Mor yw gwann heno
    Gwedy agheu Eluan,
    Ac eryr Kyndrwyn, Kyndylan.

59. Nyt angheu Ffreuer a'm de heno.
    Am damorth brodyrde
    Duhunaf, wylaf uore.

60. Nyt angheu Ffreuer a'm gwna heint
    O dechreu nos hyt deweint.
    Duhunaf, wylaf bylgeint.

61. Nyt angheu Ffreuer a'm tremyn heno;
    A'm gwna grudyeu melyn
    A choch dagreu dros erchwyn.

62. Nyt angheu Ffreuer a erniwaf heno,
    Namyn my hun yn wanglaf.
    Vym brodyr a'm tymyr a gwynaf.

63. Ffreuer wenn, brodyr a'th uaeth.
    Ny hannoedynt o'r diffaeth,
    Wyr ny uegynt vygylaeth.

64. Ffreuer wenn, brodyr a'th uu.
    Pann glywynt gywrenin llu
    Ny echyuydei ffyd ganthu.

65. Mi a Ffreuer a Medlan —
    Kyt ytuo cat ym bop mann,
    Ny'n tawr; ny ladawr an rann.

'Herding'

66. Y mynyd kyt atuo vch
    Nyt eidigafaf y dwyn vym buch.
    Ys ysgawn gan rei vy ruch.

'Newid Byd'

69. Kynn bu vyg kylchet croenen gauyr galet,
    Chwannawc y gelyn,
    Ry'm goruc y uedw ued Brynn.

70. Kynn bu vyg kylchet croenen gauyr galet,
    Kelyngar y llillen,
    Ry'm goruc y uedw ued Trenn.

71. Gwedy vym brodyr o dymyr Hafren
    Y am dwylan Dwyryw
    Gwae vi, Duw, vy mot yn vyw.

72. Gwedy meirch hywed a chochwed dillat,
    A phluawr [mawr] melyn
    Mein uyg coes: ny'm oes dudedyn.

'Gyrthmyl'

76. Bei gwreic Gyrthmwl bydei gwan hediw.
    Bydei bann y disgyr.
    Hi gyua; diua y gwyr.

'Ercal'

77. Tywarchen Ercal ar erdywal wyr
    O etiued Moryal.
    A gwedy ry's mac, ry's mal.

'Heledd'

78. Heled hwyedic y'm gelwir.
    O Duw, padiw yt rodir
    Meirch vym bro[dyr] ac eu tir?

79. Heled hwyedic a'm kyueirch. O Duw,
    Padiw yt rodir gurumseirch
    Kyndylan a'e bedwardeg meirch.

'Syllu'

80. Neur sylleis olygon ar dirion dir
    O Orsed Orwynnyon.
    Hir hwyl heul; hwy vyghouyon.

81. Neur sylleis [olygon] o Dinlleu Ureconn,
    Ffreuer werydre.
    Hiraeth am damorth vrodyrde.

....

'Broder Heledd'

83. Llas vym brodyr ar vnweith:
    Kynan, Kynndylan, Kynnwreith,
    Yn amwyn Tren, tref diffeith.

84. Ny sanghei wehelyth ar nyth Kyndylan.
    Ny thechei droetued vyth.
    Ny uagas y uam uab llyth.

85. Brodyr a'm bwyat, ny vall,
    A dyuynt ual gwyal coll.
    O vn y un edynt oll.

86. Brodyr a'm bwyat a duc Duw ragof.
    Vy anffawt a'e goruc.
    Ny obrynynt ffaw yr ffuc.

'Rhychau'

87. Teneu awel; tew lletkynt.
    Pereid y rycheu. Ny phara a'e goreu.
    [Tru] ar a uu nat ydynt.

....

'Caranfael'

91. Ny [wn y] ae nywl ae mwc
    Ae ketwyr yn kyuamwc.
    Ygweirglawd aer yssyd drwc.

92. Edeweis y weirglawd aer.
    Ysgwyt digyuyng, dinas y gedyrn,
    Goreu gwr Garanmael.

93. Karanmael, kymwy arnat.
    Atwen dy ystle o gat.
    Gnawt man ar gran kyniuiat.

94. Kymwed ognaw, llaw hael,
    Mab Kynndylan clot auael. Dywedwr
    Kynndrwynin Caranmael.

95. Oed diheid ac oed [dihat].
    Oed diholedic tref tat a geissyws
    Caranmael yn ynat.

96. Karanmael kymwed ognaw,
    Mab Kyndylan clot arllaw. Nyt ynat
    Kyt mynnat ohonaw.

97. Pan wisgei Garanmael gatpeis Gynndylan
    A phrydyaw y onnen
    Ny chaffei Ffranc tanc o'e benn.

'Heledd a'i Brawd Claf'

98. Amser y bum vras vwyt
    Ny dyrchafwn vy mordwyt
    Yr gwr a gwynei claf gornwyt.

99. Brodyr a'm bwyat inneu —
    Ny's cwynei gleuyt cornnwydeu:
    Vn Eluan; Kyndylan deu.

100. Ny mat wisc briger ny'w dirper o wr
     Yn diruawr gywryssed.
     Nyt oed leuawr vym broder.

101. Onyt rac agheu ac aeleu mawr,
     A gloes glas uereu
     Ny bydaf leuawr inneu.

....

'Tren'

104. Pedwarpwnn broder a'm bu
     Ac y bob un penn teulu.
     Ny wyr Tren perchen ydu.

105. Pedwarpwnn broder a'm buant
Ac y bop un gorwyf nwyvant.
Ny wyr Tren perchen keugant.

106. Penwarpwn terwyn o adwyn vrodyr
A'm buant o Gyndrwyn.
Nyt oes y Drenn berchen mwyn.

'Chwiorydd Heledd'

107. Amser y buant addfwyn
Y cerid merched Cyndrwyn,
Heledd, Gwladus a Gwenddwyn.

108. Chwiorydd a'm by ddidan.
Mi a'i collais oll achlan:
Ffreuer, Medwyl a Medlan.

109. Chwiorydd a'm bu hefyd.
Mi a'i collais oll i gyd:
Gwledyr, Meysir a Cheinfryd.

IV

'Llym Awel'

1. Llym awel; llum brin. Anhaut caffael clid.
   Llicrid rid; reuhid llin.
   Ry seiw gur ar vn conin.

2. Ton tra thon toid tu tir.
   Goruchel guaetev rac bron banev bre.
   Breit allan orseuir.

3. Oer [guely] lluch rac brythuch gaeaw.
   Crin [calaw; caun] truch.
   Kedic awel; coed in i bluch.

4. Oer guely pisscaud yg kisscaud iaen.
   Cul hit; caun barywhaud.
   Birr diuedit; guit gvyrhaud.

5. Ottid eiry, guin y cnes.
   Nid a kedwir o'e neges.
   Oer llinnev; eu llyu heb tes.

6. Ottid eiry; guin aren.
   Segur yscuid ar iscuit hen.
   Ry uaur guint; reuhid dien.

7. Ottid eiry ar warthaw reo.
   Gosgupid guint blaen guit tev.
   Kadir yscuid ar yscuit glev.

8. Ottid eiry, tohid istrad.
   Diuryssint vy keduir y cad.
   Mi nid aw; anaw ni'm gad.

9. Ottid eiry o dv riv,
   Karcharaur goruit; cul biv.
   Nid annuyd hawdit hetiv.

10. Ottid eiry; guin goror mynit.
    Llum guit llog ar mor.
    Meccid llvwyr llauer kyghor.

11. Eurtirn am cirn, cirn am cluir.
    Oer llyri; lluchedic auir.
    Bir diwedit; blaen gvit gvir.

12. Gvenin igogaur; guan gaur adar.
    Dit diulith……………………..
    K[a]ssulwin kewin brin; coch gwaur.

13. Guenin igodo; oer agdo rid.
    Reuid rev pan vo.
    Ir nep goleith lleith dyppo.

14. Guenin ig keithiv; gwirtliv mor.
    Crin calaw; caled riv.
    Oer divlit yr eluit hetiv.

15. Guenin ig clidur rac gulybur gaeaw.
    Glas cunlleit; cev ewur.
    Dricweuet llyvrder ar gur.

16. Hir nos, llum ros, lluid riv.
    Glas glan; guilan in emriv.
    Garv mir: glau a uit hetiv.

17. Sich guint; gulip hint; ki[u]uetlauc diffrint.
    Oer callet; cul hit.
    Llyw in awon: hinon uit.

18. Driccin imynit; avonit igniw.
    Gulichid lliw llaur trewit.
    Neut gueilgi gueled ir eluit.

19. Nid vid iscolheic, nid vid eleic unben,
    Ny'th eluir in dit reid.
    Och, Gindilic, na buost gureic.

20. Kirchid carv crum tal cum clid.
    Briuhid ia; brooet llum.
    Ry dieigc glev o lauer trum.

21. Bronureith breith bron.
    Breith bron bronureith.
    Briuhid tal glan gan garn carv culgrum cam.
    Goruchel awel guaetvann.
    Breit, guir, orseuir allan.

22. Kalan gaeaw, gurim gordugor blaen gruc.
    Goreuynauc ton mor.
    Bir dit. Deruhid ych kighor.

23. O kiscaud yscuid a[r] aral goruit
    A guir deur diarchar
    Tec nos y ffisscau escar.

24. Kinteic guint; creilum coed.
    Crin caun; caru iscun.
    Pelis enuir, pa tir hun?

25. Kin ottei eiry hid in Aruul Melin
    Ni'm gunaei artu awirtul.
    Towissun e lv y Brin Tytul.

26. Can medrit mor ruit <y> rodwit a rid —
    A[r] riv eiry a diguit —
    Pelis, pan vid kyvarwit?

27. Ni'm guna pryder im Pridein heno
    Kyrchu bro priw Uchei[n]
    Y ar can kanlin Owein.

28. Kin imtuin ariweu ac yscuid arnad,
    Diffreidad kad Kynuid,
    Pelis, pa tir y'th uaguid?

29. Y gur a rithao Duv o ri gaeth carchar,
    Rut y par o penaeth,
    Owein Reged a'm ry vaeth.

30. Can ethiv ruiw in rod[wi]t iwerit
    A teulu, na fouch.
    Guydi met meuil na vynuch.

31. Y bore gan las y dit
    Ban kirchuid Mug Maur Treuit
    Nyd oet uagaud meirch Mechit.

32. Ni'm guna lleuenit llad
    O'r chuetleu a'm diallad:
    Mechit, golo guit arnad.

33. Kyuaruuan am cavall.
    Kelein aruiar ar wall —
    Kywranc Run a'r drud arall.

34. Canis fonogion Mugc a lataut Mechit,
    Drudwas, ni's amgiffredit,
    Periw New, pereiste imi dyuit.

35. Gwir igrid; rid rewittor,
    Oeruelauc tonn; brith bron mor.
    Ren, rothid duvin kighor.

36. Mechit mab Llywarch, dihawarch vnben,
    Glvystec llen, lliw alarch,
    Kyntaw a ffruinclymus march.

Appendix:
Partially Modernized Version of the First Ten Stanzas

1. Llym awel; llwm bryn. Anhawdd caffael clyd.
   Llygrid rhyd; rhewid llyn.
   Rhy seif gwr ar un conyn.

2. Ton tra thon toid tu tir.
   Goruchel gwaeddeu rhag bron banneu bre.
   Breidd allan orsefir.

3. Oer lle llwch rhag brythwch gaeaf.
   Crin cawn; calaf trwch.
   Cedig awel; coed yn eu blwch.

4. Oer gwely pyscawd yng nghysgawd iaën.
   Cul hydd; cawn baryfawd.
   Byr diwedydd; gwydd gwyrawd.

5. Otid eiry, gwyn ei gnes.
   Nid a cedwyr o'e neges.
   Oer llynneu; eu lliw heb des.

6. Otid eiry; gwyn aren.
   Segur ysgwyd ar ysgwydd hen.
   Rhy fawr gwynt; rhewid dien.

7. Otid eiry ar warthaf rhew.
   Gosgupid gwynt blaen gwydd tew.
   Cadr ysgwyd ar ysgwydd glew.

8. Otid eiry; toid ystrad.
   Difrysynt cedwyr i gad.
   Mi nid af; anaf ni'm gad.

9. Otid eiry o du rhiw.
   Carcharawr gorwydd; cul biw.
   Nid anwyd hafddydd heddiw.

10. Otid eiry; gwyn goror mynydd.
    Llwm gwydd llong ar for.
    Mecid llwfyr llawer cyngor.

NOTES

I

1 This stanza is found only in the 17th c. manuscript of John Davies, Mallwyd, NLW 4973B. It is the last verse found only in that manuscript of a poem, 'Gwahodd Llywarch i Lanfawr', but the stanza is also written into the copy of the Red Book *englynion* found later in NLW 4973B in this position at the beginning of the dialogue. There is some evidence that the Red Book copy was collated with at least one other copy of the *englynion*, now lost, which could be a source for this verse being the first verse of the dialogue between Llywarch and Gwên. However, the similarity of *Rodwydd Forlas* in this stanza to *ryt uorlas* named twice in the *marwnad* to Gwên may have been sufficient for the antiquary, John Davies, to insert the stanza from his earlier copy in the same manuscript. While it could be argued that this is a stray verse from the time before Gwên's return home, inclusion in the poem makes a good deal of sense, and it appears to motivate Gwên's first speech. If the verse is included each speaker is allotted seven verses, with Llywarch as expected beginning the exchange, and Gwên more unexpectedly getting the last word.

a This opening line, like 2b, is a nominal sentence, sometimes called a copula zero sentence. The telegraphic style of the nominal sentence can be difficult to spot initially. Great succinctness and enhanced metrical effects are gained by the stylistic omission of the verb 'to be' in such phrases. Read: 'Thin is my shield'. While the order of adjective followed by a noun may occasionally be found in poetry and lenition in this reversal is not always shown in the mss., a nominal sentence in the *englynion* should be considered: cf. *gwlyb gro*, not 'wet gravel' (which if mutation was shown although it isn't always would be *gwlyb ro*) but 'wet [is the] gravel'. It might help to familiarize yourself with the nominal sentence by turning short descriptive sentences into this pattern stage by stage: 'The sky is blue' > 'Blue is the sky' > 'Blue the sky' > 'Blue sky'. 'His car is red' > 'Red is his car' > 'Red his car'.

b **Cybwyf:** The concessive conjunction *cy(d)* is attested compounded with forms of *bod;* the expected spelling would be *cyfwyf.*

as gallaf: *As* could be an orthographic variant of *os*, the conjunction *o* + 3rd sg. infixed object pronoun. However, with the concessive conjunction in the preceding clause, it is better to take this either as the syllabic form of the 3rd sg. object pronoun, or the particle *a* used as a preverbal particle to infix the object pronoun.

rodwydd orlas: ms. Rodwydd Forlas. In the following *marwnad* to Gwên, Llywarch states he kept watch on Llawen (15–17), best explained as a river name, and also that Gwên kept watch *ygoror ryt uorlas* (19), and was killed at *ryt vorlas* (23). From at least the eighteenth century this was assumed to refer to Morlas brook near the Shropshire border in Powys, and Llawen was taken awkwardly as an alternative name for the stream. In questioning the Powys origins of the Llywarch Hen cycle, Patrick Sims-Williams argues the only place-name in the poem is Llawen, and that in all instances *uorlas/Forlas/vorlas* are errors for an original colour adjective **uorlas* 'very green', as in 15c *ar glawd gorlas*. Normally we would expect to see dissimilation of **uorlas* to **orlas*, as in 15c, but the scribes seem to have interpreted the word after *ryt* and *rodwydd* as Morlas. (For the mutation of a proper noun in the genitive after f. sg. noun, see GMW, p. 14.) See further, 'The Provenance of the Llywarch Hen Poems: A Case for Llan-gors, Brycheiniog', CMCS 26 (1993), pp. 42–44.

Rhodwydd seems to have been a special type of ford. It is found in place-names, sometimes interchangeably with *rhyd*, as seems to be the case in this instance. Although single combat at a ford is attested in Celtic literature, there is no need to assume that the night watch would be undertaken by a single person. Fords were places to guard against the passage of raiders, who would be unlikely to take up the challenge of one hero against another. The *marwnad* does not mention other defenders, but the grieving father concentrates solely on the deeds of his lost son.

c **gwiliaf**: For *gwyliaf*, with *i* for *y* as in the Black Book orthography.

2a **vit vrwyn**: *Bit* is the 3rd sg. imperative of *bod*. For the lenition of the predicate, probably the norm but not always indicated in MW orthography, see GMW, p. 19. The order of copula + predicate + subject found here is usual in the early period; see GMW, pp. 139–40. Alternatively *vit* could be an orthographic variation of the 2nd sg. imperative, *vyd*, with *brwyn dy vryt* a phrase modifying the subject 'sad as regards your mind, low-spirited'; see GMW, p. 37.

b **Llem awel**: The two phrases in this line are nominal sentences; cf. 1a. In this type of nominal sentence the definite article before the subject is usually omitted. The apparent agreement between subject and predicate is not usual in a nominal sentence. *Llem* here probably preserves a common older orthography of -e̯- for -y̯-, with the scribes seeing initially a f. singular adjective modifying a f. singular noun, and thus failing to regularize to their own orthographic system. The nominal sentence, in fact, occurs as expected in the opening words of another saga poem, 'Llym awel'; see IV.1a. See further, T. Arwyn Watkins, 'The

Descriptive Predicative in Old and Middle Welsh', pp. 287–88. The biting wind could be a literal description of the night's weather, or meant to convey the emotional atmosphere of coldness and piercing disdain.

chwerw gwenwyn: The second nominal sentence is gnomic. Gnomes, statements about what is usual, common or unvarying, are used throughout the dialogue, with much of the verbal battle between son and father fought obliquely through these statements. The gnome, *chwerw gwenwyn*, probably refers to bitterness of familial ill-feeling. Both words have a wide range of figurative meanings which are more relevant here than the literal. *Chwerw* 'bitter' can also mean 'painful, hurtful', and *gwenwyn*, primarily 'poison', is best taken here as 'bad feeling, bitterness, ill-will'.

c **Amgyhud:** This could be either a compound of *am* + *cyhuddo*, as the lenited ms. form suggests, or (less likely) *a'm cyhud* < *a* + 1st sg. dative infixed pronoun with the lenition a scribal error. Either one makes sense here. In MnW *cyhuddo* is 'to accuse', but medieval meanings include 'to declare, assert, make known'. This is a somewhat ironic assertion by Gwên of his filial bond to Llywarch, and therefore his duty — presumably his mother's word on his paternity can be trusted. The subordinate clause, *mab yt wyf*, is simply juxtaposed, unlike later MW which would, like Modern Welsh, use a *bod* clause.

Note the rhyme in this stanza. Lenited /m/ originally had a strong nasal element which allowed it for a time to be distinguished from lenited /b/ in early Old Welsh orthography in which the lenited sounds were often represented by the radical. The stanza before the loss of the nasal element would have had generic rhyme of final nasals. This is probably an early feature.

3a **Neut:** *Neu, neud* before vowels, is a common preverbal particle, and *neud* is also used for the copula. It introduces a strongly affirmative sentence, 'indeed …, truly …'.

atwen ar: *Atnabot ar* 'to know from observation of'.

awen: This is a rare usage of *awen* as other than 'poetic inspiration', despite the later attribution of the poetry to Llywarch. The use of the more general sense corresponds to the general lack of references to the bards in the early *englynion*. Compare the similar statement from *Culhwch ac Olwen* discussed below.

b **Yn hanuot:** Literally: 'I know of our coming from': 'that we come from'; cf. the clause in 2c. Arthur similarly says in *Culhwch* that shared lineage speaks to the heart and intuition: CO 166–67 *Mae uyg kallon yn tirioni vrthyt. Mi a wn dy hanuot o'm gvaet.* 'My heart is growing tender towards you. I know you come from my blood line.' In *Culhwch* Arthur does not yet know the identity of his kinsman, but the situation here may not be identical. Gwên has stated he has the obligation to take over the duties of his failing father, assuming his mother's declaration on his paternity is trustworthy. Llywarch acknowledges that his heart is in no doubt on the matter — in part, of course, because Gwên has just expressed willingness to go to battle. He therefore must be a chip off the old block. As is usual in this dialogue, Llywarch's positive words to Gwên are followed by qualifications or doubts.

c **Trigwyd**: Impersonal preterite indicative of *trigo* 'to stay, dwell, remain, delay'. This line could be taken with the previous one, speaking of Llywarch's bloodline, but the brevity implied by the diminutive *oric* does not go with a boast of long and distinguished ancestry. Also possible is a true impersonal, 'someone has tarried' (lit. 'there has been a tarrying'), which is typical of Llywarch's often indirect criticism of his son. Final d̲ for /d/, however, is rare in the mss. It is perhaps best to take this as an error for *trigyd*, 2nd sg. pres./fut. indicative, 'you tarry, you delay', a direct attack on Gwên's supposed reluctance to go to battle. For the form, see GMW, p. 115 and below, 5a *diegyd*.

oric elwic: *Oric* is a diminutive of *awr* in the sense of 'time' rather than literally 'an hour'. *Elwic* is an adjectival formation from *elw* 'benefit, profit'. Together: 'a precious while, a valuable space of time'. Gwên is accused unfairly of being less than eager to fight.

a Wen: In MW orthography the combination of the vocative particle *a* (leniting) + Gwên is identical to the rhyme word of line a, word play also evident orally despite the difference in vowel length. Gwên (with a long vowel and a single *n* in earlier orthography) should not be confused with the feminine name, Gwen (a short vowel and two *n*'s). The personal name is probably from the common noun meaning 'smile, laughter'.

4a **ygryt**: There are many ways of representing the nasal mutation after *yn* in MW. The orthography here cannot be split when showing modern word division. It corresponds to *yng ngryd* in Modern Welsh spelling.

b **Armaaf**: *Ar-ma-af* (3 syllables), also in 10b.

c **Kynnyt**: from *cyd* + *ny(d)*.

Duw gennyt: Lit. 'God [be] with you', a way of saying 'goodbye'. Gwên may hope to escape further tongue-lashing from his father.

5a **a'th**: The preverbal particle *a* serves to infix the object pronoun; GMW, p. 172.

welif: The ending of the 1st sg. pres./fut. indicative of i-stem verbs was *-if*. The form survives in poetry up to the earlier Poets of the Princes, usually in rhyming position (as here), and was also added to non i-stem verbs. See GMW, p. 115 and Rodway, *Dating Medieval Welsh Literature*, pp. 45–47.

b **o'th ry ledir**: For the various usages of the pre-verbal particle *ry*, see GMW, pp. 166–69. The compound *or* < *o + ry* is attested, used before the present and future tenses. It would seem to underline the uncertainty of the possible future event (GMW, pp. 168, 241). However, *ry* sometimes appears not to have any particular force (but without it here the line would be short). Note the parallel line has simply *o diegyd*. In earlier usage the infixed pronoun might be expected with *ry*; cf. IV.29c.

gwynif: See above on *welif*.

ar gnif: *Gnif* 'feat, work' like many similar words can be used figuratively for 'battle'; *ar gnif* 'in battle'. The mss. have a variant, *er gnif*, which would change the meaning slightly, 'despite battle'. There is often confusion or variation between *yr, ar, er*; cf. below, 6b.

6a **Ny chollaf dy wyneb**: The simple addition of *dy* indicates Gwên is well aware of his father's true concerns, for his own fame earned vicariously through his sons.

trinwosep wr: This epithet must be ironic applied to Llywarch who at the start was arming himself so feebly, unless it refers to his readiness to provoke conflict by goading with his tongue.

b **y'r ystre**: As is frequent a verb of motion is implied by the preposition: '[to go] to the border'. The mss. have a variant *ar ystre* which in this case makes less sense since the first two verses of the dialogue indicate arming oneself was done before departing for the border watch.

c **Porthaf gnif**: The expression occurs as a gnome in another saga poem, 'Geraint fab Erbin': *porthit gnif bob kyniuiat* ('every warrior endures hardship'.)

mudif lle: *Mudo* is the simple verb compounded in MnW *symud, ymfudo*. For the form, see above 5a. The rhyme facilitated here is internal with *gnif*. *Mudo lle* from the context appears to be 'to give ground, yield ground to the enemy.' The promise to fight to a certain point is conditional, but none the less heroic. Llywarch, the proponent of the extremes of heroism, does not object to this vow as such in the next verse, he only casts doubt on Gwên's resolve to fulfil it.

7a The opening gnome here describes nature; gnomes are usually classified as nature gnomes or human gnomes, those concerned with human behaviour. The description of a free-flowing wave in the absence of any obstacles may be intended by Llywarch to reflect doubt on Gwên's promises to bear battle hardship once real difficulty is encountered.

b **Ech adaf**: *Ech* 'from, out' is a rare preposition cognate with Latin *ex*. While *ech adaf* 'from the hand' and *ech y aghat* 'from his hand' are attested, here it seems to be part of a non-literal expression based on 'hand', like many others in Welsh, although *llaw* is the word more usually used; cf. *ar y llaw arall, maes o law,* etc. The precise meaning is unclear. From the context, 'quickly, later, casually' would all suit. English 'out of hand' can be compared.

torrit: The 3rd sg. pres./fut. indicative of simple (non-compound) verbs in Welsh preserves the old Celtic verbal distinction between absolute and conjunct. Conjunct forms are used after any pre-verbal particle, and absolute when the verb stands independently. For a full discussion, see Rodway, *Dating Medieval Welsh Literature*, pp. 85–116. With a few exceptions absolute forms are used consistently where they would be expected in the saga *englynion*. Although an adverbial phrase comes before the verb here the lack of initial position of the verb can probably be put down to poetic syntax which requires *aruaeth* in rhyming position; see further below 21a.

The absolute 3rd sg. present is often found in gnomic and proverbial statements, sometimes with a balancing negative statement which highlights the formal difference between absolute and conjunct; cf. III.87b *pereid y rycheu. ny phara ae goreu.* ('The furrows remain; those who made them do not.') The frequent use of the 3rd sg. absolute forms in gnomic statements at times lends an air of the habitual to them. This is clearly the case here where Llywarch is making an assertion about the common behaviour of those who make an heroic vow (*aruaeth*). *Ech adaf torrit aruaeth* should be seen as a gnome, just like line c *gnawt ffo ar ffraeth* which has the common gnomic formula *gnawt*. All three gnomes are aimed obliquely at Gwên. His direct response in the next verse shows he is aware of this.

c **Kat agdo**: This is a parenthetic comment (or *sangiad* in Welsh) relevant to the main theme. The warrior who is *kat agdo* would be the opposite of the heroes praised as protective pillars or fortresses in battle.

gnawt ffo ar ffraeth: This line appears in medieval proverb lists. A proportion of the gnomes and proverbs in these lists occur the saga *englynion* and some appear to be metrical in origin, from lost verse. The gnome may have been coined here in the traditional manner. For the sentiment of doubt about those who boast in the security of the feast, cf. the Old English *Battle of Maldon*, ll. 200–01 '… many spoke boldly there who later would not endure in need.' Honour depended on fulfilling vows. Because it was better to fulfil a limited vow with honour, heroic literature often cautions against making too expansive a promise, and most particularly against the tendency for a young, hot-headed warrior to make such an error. Note how in the course of this dialogue Llywarch takes the opposite course, pushing Gwên by his supposed doubts into ever greater promises of foolhardy bravery.

8a Yssit ym a lauarwyf: For *yssit*, the impersonal form of *ys*, see GMW, p. 142. 'I have (lit. there is to me) that which I may say', i.e. 'I can do whatever I may state.' The expressions used for possession in early Welsh poetry differ from later usage of *bod* + *gan*. The conjugated preposition *i* is employed here and *i* was probably used with nouns although there are few examples (cf. III.106c *nyt oes y drenn berchen mwyn*). By far the most common syntax for possession in the saga *englynion* is *bod* + an infixed dative pronoun; cf. 25–27 below. The relative pronoun is the object of the clause with the clause itself what Gwên possesses.

b **Briwaw**: The orthography is ambiguous. Either the *briwaw* is the vn '[there will be] breaking of spears', or is irregular orthography for the 1st sg. pres./fut. indicative, *briwaf*.

parth: *Parth* introduces an adverbial clause; GMW 66–67.

c **na ffowyf**: A subordinate negative clause of indirect speech ; GMW 174. The full import is not clear here. Either Gwên will not rule out tactical retreat at this point, or he will not be goaded by his father into making an admission which is beneath him. Clearly the statement is not unheroic, since Llywarch, the unyielding representative of the extreme, does not express any displeasure in his son's statement. His response is once again to question whether Gwên's heroic promise will be kept.

9a Medal migned; kalet riw: The nature gnomes or description here are apposite to Llywarch's theme of uncertain dependability. Both landscape features present solid-looking surfaces, but only one is actually firm. Both elements of landscape have further relevant connotations: the swamp as low-lying, soft and treacherous and the slope as high and solid.

b **Rac carn cann tal glann a vriw**: This illustration is similar to that of line a. Presumably the solid-seeming edge of an undercut bank is meant, an edge which will crumble when put under pressure. A descriptive adjective alone is often used poetically for a horse, as here.

It is interesting to compare a very similar line in IV.21c, B*ruihid tal glan gan garn carv culgrum cam* ('The edge of a bank is broken by the hoof of a thin, crooked, bent stag'). There is no difference in stress in the sentence as it occurs here. The particle *a* is used here in order to place the verb in final position with the rhyming conjunct form, giving a sentence structure identical to what is known as the 'abnormal sentence' pattern in Middle Welsh prose. However, early poets typically exploit the many different verbal forms and syntactical patterns available in the language for metrical reasons or variety.

c **Edewit ny wnelher ny diw**: This proverb is found in two medieval proverb lists, and is also incorporated in 'Englynion y Clyweit'. Note that *ny* is usually used in relative clauses in MW; see GMW, p. 173.

10 This stanza makes sense as it stands. However, the stanza looks like it should be an *englyn penfyr*, and if so, line a is very short. One or more words may be missing but there is insufficient evidence to make an emendation.

a **Gwasgarawt**: One of the mss. has the alternative reading, *gwasgarawc*, which would suggest the word is an adj., although only *gwasgar* is attested as such. It is better seen as the 3rd sg. pres./fut. indicative of the verb, *gwasgaru*; see GMW, p. 119.

c **brwyt briw**: No lenition is shown after the f. sg. noun, *ysgwyt*. Lenition is not invariably shown in the medieval mss. The mss. have *bryt*.

11a **corn**: *Corn*, basically an animal horn, is used both for a drinking horn and a musical instrument made from a horn. From Llywarch's instructions this would be some sort of war or hunting horn. The medieval Welsh laws attest to the use of horns for signalling, and also suggest they have high status, as would befit a gift given to Gwên by the powerful king, Urien.

Vryen: Urien Rheged, one of the leaders of the old Northern British kingdoms, is one of the best-known figures in Welsh tradition. He is the subject of early bardic poetry attributed to Taliesin, and also of an *englyn* saga about his betrayal and death which is linked to the Llywarch cycle. In the genealogies Urien is Llywarch's first cousin; see below 23b. Presumably Gwên received this gift while in fosterage or military service with his kinsman.

b **arwest eur am y en**: With a warhorn this could either be a cord attached around the mouthpiece for carrying it or a band of ornament around the mouthpiece. The latter seems more likely since a cord would require another mounting place as well and since a protective or decorative band is more likely to be *eur* 'golden, ornamental'. See also the discussion of IV.11a.

c Llywarch seemingly indicates Gwên should use the horn to call for reinforcements. In fact, it seems to be a final test of the extent to which Gwên's good sense has been undermined by his father's goading. The scornful refusal to contemplate this in stanza 12 is exactly what Llywarch has been encouraging. Ultimately it is not beneficial behaviour for either the warrior or his threatened community. This recalls the heroic dilemma in *Le Chanson de Roland*.

12c **duhunaf**: The verb is a compound of *di-* (neg.) and *huno*. The initial vowel has been assimilated to the following one.

13 Once again, although the stanza makes sense the metrics suggest a word is missing. The rhyme of *draw/gottoew/waew* is not acceptable. An *englyn penfyr* can be restored by adding an adj. such as *hoew* or *gloew* after *gwas*, or another descriptive adjective which would give proper length, since rhyme on the *gwant* is not required. *Proest* is rare in general, and not certainly attested in an *englyn*

penfyr. This suggests the older form *(g)woew* should be read for *(g)waew* in line c.

b **o eur y ottoew**: The normal order, *y ottoew o eur*, has been reversed for rhyme. This brief description along with the gilded war horn gives an impression of the splendour of the young warrior's equipment, and indicates he rode to battle. There is no indication whether or not he fought on horseback like the *Gododdin* warriors.

c **re ruthrwn**: In early poetry no particle is required between the fronted adverb and the verb.

y waew: Either Llywarch in his youth rushed to pick up his spear to go to fight, or rushed towards the enemy's spear, the more likely interpretation. He implies in this aside Gwên has been reluctant to go to battle in comparison with his father in his prime. It provokes a furious response from Gwên, who was intended to hear it. Although placed in the wrong initially by Llywarch, he agreed to take up the fight immediately, and in stanza 4 tried to depart.

14a **waes**: *Gwaës* is disyllabic. This *milwr* stanza has *proest* rhyme. *Proest* is attested but rare in the *englyn milwr*. The later 4-line equivalent most commonly has *proest* varying in all four lines; see the Introduction.

Ti yn vyw: For the syntax, see GMW, p. 140. The subject comes before the predicate in copula zero sentences when it is a personal pronoun, reversing the usual order seen in 2b, etc.

c **Ny bu eidyl hen yn was**: This line has a gnomic feel, and does appear in one of the medieval proverb lists. If *eidyl hen* is taken as a substantive compound this would look like a late type of copula sentence using *yn* before the predicate, but this construction is not otherwise attested in the early *englynion*, and the concept 'the feeble-old one was not (never) a youth', i.e. has forgotten what is was to be young, looks rather modern. It is best to take the *yn* here as *yn* + lenition in phrases indicating a state of being: 'as a youth'; cf. *yn vyw* line b above. This gives the copula syntax of (negative preverb), copula, predicate, subject. See T. Arwyn Watkins, 'The Descriptive Predicative in Old and Middle Welsh', pp. 288–89.

In light of the statement in line b that all the witnesses to Llywarch's deeds have been killed the description is more two-edged than it might at first appear. These witnesses according to medieval Welsh law cannot have been his dispatched enemies, so it must refer to his contemporaries or elders. It could be taken as solely complimentary: Llywarch has survived to old age because of his superior valour. But there is a strong suggestion, especially with the overstated confidence in Llywarch's truthfulness in line a, that the old, in the absence of witnesses to contradict them, can freely embroider on the past. Since neither his contemporaries nor his other sons have survived despite supposedly doing less than Llywarch did in his youth, it suggests his heroism was not as extreme as he now makes it out to be. Given the oblique sparring, this is not an open assertion of disbelief, but Gwên gets the last word, doubting his father's deeds just as his own courage has been called into question in the dialogue.

'Marwnad Gwên'

The *marwnad* to Gwên, the lamenting promised by his father in stanza 5 of the dialogue if he proved worthy, follows immediately in the manuscripts. Possibly a prose account would have separated the two in some performances, but all the important information about Gwên's last fight can be deduced from the poetry itself. There is probably a deliberate metrical link (*cymeriad*) between in end of stanza 14 of the dialogue and the beginning of the *marwnad* (the alliteration of *(g)was/Gwen* and rhyme between *hen, Gwen, Lawen*). The *marwnad* is a recognized bardic praise genre to a dead patron, but in the saga verse, a relative or friend performs the formal lament.

15a **Llawen**: Llawen is a place-name, most probably of the river or stream where the defensive bank (15c) and ford (1c, 19b, 23b) are located. Patrick Sims-Williams (see stanza 1c above) suggests it may be Llawennant near Brecon (p. 42).

yd welas: The mutation of the following verb in stanzas 15–17 and the use before a consonant indicate this is the leniting preverbal particle *yt*, although *yd* is the normal orthography of the Red Book for another particle /əð/ which does not cause mutation. *Yt* is used in positive sentences and clauses, both proper and improper, and is a simple affirmative particle. It is replaced by *a* in the variant of the opening verbal *cymeriad* in stanza 19. *Gwelas* for *gwylas* shows confusion copying from a different orthographic system in the first instance of the phrase, one which had *e* for /ə/. Note the exploitation of the various endings of the s-preterite (GMW, pp. 122–23) in the four instances of this opening *cymeriad*. It indicates how the poets used the full range of forms available in the language for variety and change of rhyme schemes.

neithwyr: Often an adverb of time is used in the position of the *gair cyrch* giving a sense of dramatic immediacy to the character's lament. *Hediw* and *heno* are also common in this position.

b **Yr athuc**: Again older orthography has mystified the scribes; the usual orthography would be *aduc*. *Yr* is not in the mss. but was suggested by J. E. Caerwyn Williams, BBCS 21 (1964), pp. 26–27. It gives good sense and better length. The copyist of the exemplar may have skipped *yr* because the previous word, *neithwyr*, ends in *yr*.

ny techas: Modern Welsh uses two different mutations after *ni*, aspirate mutation of /c,p,t/ and lenition of the remaining lenitable consonants. This probably reflects a difference in mutation after *ny* in early Welsh depending on whether it was in a main clause, proper relative clause (leniting relative clause), or other subordinate clause. How long this distinction continued in a meaningful fashion is uncertain because mutation was very rarely shown in OW, and sometimes is not indicated in Middle Welsh orthography. Where mutation is shown after *ny* one gets the impression the scribes are guessing or inconsistent; sometimes different mutations are found in separate copies. Here one would expect *ny thechas* as in 19c. The whole stanza suggests uncertainty in dealing with more archaic orthography at some stage in copying.

c **ar glawd gorlas**: The adjective *gorlas* used here with *clawd* and elsewhere with *ryt* and *rodwydd* suggests some sort of fortification at a river crossing built of turf.

16b **a'r ysgwyt**: The definite article is sometimes used rather than the possessive pronoun when ownership is very clear; see GMW, p. 25, and compare 17b. However, after the conjunction a repetition the definite article would be expected rather than a switch to the 3rd sg. m. possessive pronoun; see GMW, p. 24. Comparing 17b, *a'r ysgwyt ar yr ysgwyd* should probably be restored here although the translation would still be 'his' in both cases. Alternatively in 16b *a'r ysgwyt* could be changed to *a'y ysgwyt*, a reading which is found in NLW 4973B. The pair *ysgwyt* and *ysgwyd* are common in poetry, for both assonance and sense.

c **bu mab ymi**: The use of the conjugated preposition rather than the possessive pronon distinguishes between 'my son' and 'a son of mine'.

17b **ar y gnis**: *Gnis* is the lower part of the face. The position of the shield is one of readiness. It would seem to be a description of use of a long shield, but smaller round shields are best attested in pre-Norman Wales; see Jenny Day, 'Shields in Welsh Poetry up to c. 1300: Decorations, Shape and Significance', SC 45 (2011), pp. 27–33.

18 This verse is irregular metrically, and has many difficulties of interpretation. It also appears to be out of order since 19 carries on, with slight variation, the verbal formulae of 15 and 16. Verses 18 and 20 should also go together since they mark a shift in the *marwnad* from description of Gwên in the 3rd sg. to direct apostrophe of the dead, a feature found in other saga poems as the character speaks with rising intensity.

b This line is short. *Mawr* appears to rhyme (generic) in a *penfyr* verse with *gochawd* and *ladawr* (itself uncertain). A noun could be missing modified by *mawr*: 'your death is a great x', or *ym* 'for me' could be inserted after *ys*, and *mawr* taken as modifying *casnar*. Reconstruction is made more difficult by the uncertainty of meaning of *casnar* and the rest of line c. On *ys* see further III.2a and III.18a.

c **Casnar:** *Casnar* occurs both as a personal name and common noun. It may be a compound. *Nar* 'lord' is clear enough, but it is uncertain whether the element *cas* which occurs in personal names should be associated with *cas* 'enmity, hatred, wrath'. *Casnar* is almost certainly the common noun here, for which GPC gives the meanings a) 'wrath, grief, pain' and b) 'hero, lord'.

Nyt car a'th ladawr: The ending *-awr* is future or rarely pres. impersonal indicative, and so does not make much sense. Emending to *ladawd* 3rd sg. pret. indicative would retain rhyme, but this form of the pret. is generally late, and the meaning would be very trite. This *englyn* is probably much more corrupt than it appears at first sight, and cannot be translated with certainty after *dy leas*. For further suggestions, see EWSP, pp. 519–20.

19a **vordwyt tylluras:** The descriptive phrase is lenited because it is used as an epithet; see GMW, p. 15. *Tylluras* is a compound of two similar adjectives; compare *tylluawr* in the *Gododdin*.

20b **Ruthyr eryr yn ebyr oedut:** The second vowel in *ruthyr* is epenthetic, and does not form part of the rhyming scheme. *Eryr* and *ebyr* are also linked in the *Gododdin* where the rush of the eagle is associated with swift swooping dives to feed in the estuary. Cf. also 'Geraint fab Erbin' 21–26, which compare rushing horses to eagles. The phrase must be taken as genitival: 'you were of the rush of an eagle....'

c **Betwn:** *Betwn*, *pettwn* is a contraction which is attested fairly early of *pei yt uwn* < *pei* 'if' + 1st sg. imperf. subjunctive. But *Betwn* here probably preserves older orthography for *bydwn* 1st sg. imperf. used as conditional, 'were I'.

dedwyd: The basic meanings of *dedwydd* are 'happy, fortunate, blessed'. Much of the philosophy about fate and self-determination in early poetry and wisdom literature is centred around the concept of the *dedwydd* man and his opposite, the *diriaid*. The *dedwydd* man is wise, peace-loving, and in harmony with God. His happiness and blessing ultimately stem from his character and behaviour. The *diriaid* is contentious, foolish, and sometimes wicked. He is ostracized on earth, and can expect no mercy from God. The bad fate of the *diriaid*, then, also arises from his character and how he copes with innate tendencies. In the context, Llywarch is saying far more than just if he were fortunate Gwên would not have been killed. It is his behaviour and lack of wisdom which has led to the deaths of all of his sons, not just malevolent fate.

21a **Tonn tyruit:** Note the order subject, verb with no mark of subordination. Early poetry has examples of rather free syntax. While the absolute form of the verb would be expected to be in initial position the order is probably metrically determined here. Internal rhyme and alliteration in lines of two parts are usually found around the caesura. A *nominativus pendens* construction is a possible interpretation but more forced with such a short sentence; see Rodway, *Dating Medieval Welsh Literature*, p. 109.

The breaking waves introduced in 21 and 22 are examples of nature description used to provide mood. The sound of the sea often evokes loneliness and grief in medieval Welsh verse; for further examples see Haycock, *Legendary Poems from the Book of Taliesin*, p. 463. It is not intended as a realistic description of the character's situation — most of the Welsh borderland is nowhere near the sea. This use of nature description to harmonize with or contrast with the mood of the speaker is found elsewhere in the saga poetry, sometimes changing within the poem according to the needs of emotion, not realism.

b **Pan ant kynrein**: Variants of this verse where the excluded speaker watches the departure of warriors are found elsewhere; cf. IV.8b. There are a few 'floating' verses to be found in the saga corpus, although in each case the verse is adapted according to the situation. These two verses are good examples of the incremental type of verbal repetition. Little is changed in all three lines except the rhyme words, but there is a development of meaning.

22c **ry'th golles**: The preverbal particle *ry* is used here in a relative construction, with the infixed 2nd sg. object pronoun.

23a **Oed gwr**: Llywarch in the dialogue called Gwên a *gwas* 'youth'. There is no necessary contradiction here. Llywarch may have deliberately played down Gwên's maturity in his programme to enrage him. *Gwas* could also be used affectionately for a man in his prime. However, *gwr* can also mean 'warrior', and this is probably the best sense here: three past tense copula statements showing his promise, come to nothing with Gwên's death in line c.

b **nei y**: The term *nai* in MW included the sons of first and second cousins, as well as the sons of siblings, although in the law tracts the relationship is usually qualified by expressions such as *'nei vab cevynderw'*. Llywarch was first cousin to Urien twice over according to the genealogies. The preposition *i* is used rather than a genitive with *nai*, cf. 16c.

c **llas Gwen**: On *llas*, see GMW, p. 127. This stanza marks the end of the true *marwnad* to Gwên. In the next stanzas (except for the intrusive stanza 24) Llywarch moves on to speak of his other lost sons, first by asserting Gwên was the best of them, and then to admitting his role in their deaths. By placing the word 'Gwên' in the final position this section returns full circle to the opening word at the beginning of the *marwnad*. This metrical technique, used to round off sections or entire poems, is attested elsewhere in Welsh, Irish and Anglo-Saxon verse. Note, too, how in the part of the poem lamenting Gwên his name appears in every stanza. This is a regular feature of saga *marwnadau*.

24a This verse is an obvious interpolation. The stanza, with slight variation, is found in the Black Book of Carmarthen 'Stanzas of the Graves'. Such interpolations of antiquarian interest sometimes entered texts from marginal entries during transmission. However, the changes made here to the stanza as it appears in the Black Book suggest that in this case the stanza was deliberately inserted, and altered to fit its new context. The inappropriate opening formula of the grave stanzas, *Pieu y bed* ('Whose is the grave?'), is replaced here by bardic style epithets in line a, and in addition, the opening word alliterates with the following three stanzas.

Prennyal: 'Spear-fight, battle' < *pren*, the wooden shaft of the spear used as *pars pro toto*, and *gâl* 'enmity'.

gal ysgwn: *Gâl* has a wide range of meanings, from 'enemy' to 'enmity, hatred, passion, valour'; similarly *ysgwn* 'ready, swift, bold, stubborn'. This gives a wide range as well for the phrase describing Gwên: 'of stubborn valour' or 'of ready/swift valour/enmity', etc.

b **goruc ar Lloegyr llu cyngrwn**: Although the prep. *ar* causes lenition, ll and rh resist mutation after n and r, as is still the case in MnW after *yn* and *mor*. The preposition with *gwneuthur* changes the meaning to something done against: 'inflict upon, commit against'. *Lloegyr* is both the people and the kingdom they occupy; here the people, and more specifically the men or warriors. So Gwên made the English into a compacted or huddled host.

25a **Pedwar meib ar hugeint**: *Meib* is a pl. of *mab* used only with numerals. There is some irregularity of length in the three stanzas with this opening formula which can be resolved by restoring more archaic formations for the numbers over twenty. In stanzas 25–27 the line would be regular if *ar* is omitted. There is indirect evidence for a construction like this in Cornish, and in the numbers 11–19 in Welsh. *Deuddeg* preserves this type of formation to this day, and in MW *undec* is attested vs. MnW *un ar ddeg*. For stanza 28 and 29 one can compare OIr which used *ar* to join multiples of ten in substantive numerals, cf. *dias ar fichit* 'twenty-two persons'. If early Welsh had a similar construction, we should restore '*Pedwar ar hugeint*' in 27 and 28, omitting *meib*. It would not be surprising for the more archaic formation to be changed over time, and for the verbal formula, *pedwar meib ar hugeint*, to spread to all the stanzas creating opening lines in most of the verses which are on the upper limits of attested line length, or over.

a'm bu: See above 8a.

b **Eurdorchawc**: Lit. 'adorned with a gold or valuable torque', although in the *Gododdin* which uses the adj. frequently as a substantive it appears at times to be synonymous with 'warrior'. The classic neck torque of the Celts would have long been archaic even in the sixth century. However, the word, as in Latin, was probably applied to other ornaments rather than preserving an archaism over hundreds of years. It is found in the poetry of the Poets of the Princes as well, and was also used to describe a relic of St. Cadog which was extant in the Middle Ages. The wearing of valuable jewellery in itself was an indication of wealth, and therefore nobility.

tywyssawc: *Tywysog* is an adjectival formation from *tywys* 'to lead, rule', but generally it is attested as a noun, 'prince, ruler', from the substantive usage. This is a possible use if *llu* is genitival, and line b refers to Gwên. However, it makes better sense and poetry for Llywarch to contrast his splendid sons in lines a and b with the even better Gwên in c, and therefore *tywyssawc* is best taken as a rare instance of the adj. 'princely'. This also makes for a smoother reading in 27b.

onadu: GMW, p. 59.

26c **o'e dat**: *O'e* would appear to be a form of the preposition *o* 'from', but is based on the combination of the 3rd sg. and pl. contracted possessive pronouns with *do*, the older form of *y* 'to'. The contracted forms preserved the original vowel which evolved in the simple preposition *do* to *ddy*, then *y*. See GMW, p. 53.

27a **bwyn**: This is an orthographical variant for *bwy-yn(t)*. The rhyme of the third plural verbal forms with -nn as seen here is well attested in the *englynion*. It appears that the final -t was lost early in speech, surviving in the learned language of the poets, perhaps with some influence of analogous Latin verbal endings. As is the case with other variants in the language, the poets exploit both the archaic and contemporary according to metrical need.

This flexibility is also seen in the syntax of the poetry. Stanzas 25–27, with their fronting of the predicate, would conform to the 'abnormal' sentence of Middle Welsh prose. The sentence order is variable, and no extra stress is accorded the fronted part of the sentence. Given the free order of verse, it is somewhat questionable whether the pattern here is fully analogous to the later prose sentence. The verbal particle *a* serves to infix the dative pronoun. In the sentences where *a* or *ry* appear, the question of concord between verb and subject arises. In the true relative or emphatic sentence in Middle Welsh the fronted plural subject is usually, but not invariably, followed by a 3rd sg. verb. In the 'abnormal' sentence, however, usually the verb is in the third plural. Because the usage is not totally consistent even in Middle Welsh, and because the use of the preverb may not be necessary except to infix, lack of consistency in the poetry between plural or singular alone is of doubtful significance for dating purposes. Presumably concord between plural subject and verb is the original syntax; the use of the third singular may have spread to those sentences using a preverb to infix a dative or object pronoun from similarly formed sentences with true relative construction, or simply from the usual usage of a singular verb with a plural subject in normal, verb-initial sentences. Variants of a formula such as we see here indicate that by the period of the *englynion*, if not before, both concord and lack of concord were acceptable, with the choice being heavily dependent on metrical requirements. In 25 and 26 the opening verbal formula has a singular verb and in 27 has a plural verb. All are in rhyming position. One can compare the exploitation of the various s-preterite endings in the opening stanzas of the *marwnad*.

28a **kenueint lywarch**: Llywarch is lenited because it is a proper noun in a genitival relationship with a feminine singular noun; see GMW, p. 14. Both 28a and 29a are long. Possibly *meib* should be omitted in both.

c **eu**: A variant of *yw*; cf. *pieu* 'whose is'.

29a **a ueithyeint**: At first glance this looks like a verb with the preverbal particle *a* preceeding of the same formation as the other plural passives in the verse. However, there is no preposition for the agent before *vyg knawt*, and emendation to include one would be questionable, since the line is already long. The *a* is best taken as a variant of the prep. *o*, and *meithyeint* as a derivative noun from the verb *magu* 'to nurture, raise'. This variant of the preterite stem of the verb, *maeth-*, is found in the verbal adjective compounded with *med* and *gwin*, *gwinueith*, *medueith*, in the *Gododdin*.

Verses 28 and 29 are closely linked both in subject matter and metrically. It is rare in the *englynion* poems to have two verses with the same end rhyme within the compass of a poem. When it does occur, it is invariably in two adjacent stanzas, as here, and undoubtedly forms a deliberate metrical link. Also note the internal rhymes *dyuot/clot* and *dyuot/bychot*, serving to emphasize the bitter lesson learned at last by Llywarch.

b **Drwy vyn tauawt**: That is, through the words he said. He caused their deaths, even if he was not the actual killer.

llesseint: This is a rather rare plural passive verb, used primarily when essential to distinguish between sg. and pl. where the antecedent is fronted, as in the case of *llesseint*, or not directly specified, as in *colledeint* in line c. See GMW, p. 127. The usual formation is the addition of *-eint*, a rare 3rd pl. imperfect ending (see GMW, p. 122) to the passive preterite form; cf. 23c. This is the formation of the verb in the following line. The mss. have *lledesseint*, with *-eint* added to the 3rd sg. preterite rather than to the passive preterite *llas*. This is probably a later formation, when the ending itself was seen as supplying the passive force, and it makes the line rather long.

II

The White Book copies and the independent copy in NLW 4973B, have the title 'Englynion Llywarch' here. It is the first of the poems clearly belonging to the

Llywarch Hen cycle in the manuscripts, although stanza 20 clearly shows that it post-dates the death of all his sons. This suggests that however the poetry was collected, it was not from a continuous version of the saga, whether written or recovered from oral performance. It is justifiably one of the most famous saga poems, and it can stand alone with only a little background knowledge about Llywarch and his sons. For another analysis of this poem which links it to the preceeding poem in the Red Book, usually taken as independent, see Richard Sharpe, 'Claf Abercuawg and the Voice of Llywarch Hen', SC 43 (2009), pp. 113-21.

1a **bum**: *Bum*, sometimes written *buum*, was originally disyllabic. Judging by line length there may be examples in the *englynion* of the disyllabic form (cf. IV.99a), but here and in 2a and 3a the older form would make the lines very long. It is not clear when the contracted form became current, and for how long the disyllabic form survived as a variant. For a discussion, see Marged Haycock, *Legendary Poems from the Book of Taliesin*, p. 187.

b **Keinmygyr uy eres**: *Keinmygyr* would appear to be an error for *keinmygir*, pres. indicative impersonal of *ceinmygu*. However, it could have been interpreted by a scribe as a compound of the adjectives *cain* 'fair, fine' and *mygyr* 'fine, bright', explaining the form in the manuscripts. The adjective would make the line rather short unless the epenthetic vowel in *mygyr* is counted for metrics, not generally the case.

If it is a verbal form, there is a strong case for emending to *keinmygit*, imperf. impersonal; cf. *kynwyssit* in line b of the following stanza. However, in the opening stanzas Llywarch's high opinion of his glorious youth is intact. In that case, the present tense *keinmygir* could be understood (depending on the sense of *uy eres*) as asserting his deeds are (still) admired, but this is less likely. *Eres* is only attested as an adjective 'strange, wondrous, amazing'. If *eres* could be taken as a noun, 'wondrous deeds, feat' it would make good sense, although this usage has not been accepted in GPC. Otherwise, *uy* can be taken as an error in reading minims in earlier orthography for *yn*: 'It (Llywarch's eloquence) was (also emending to *keinmygit*) wondrously admired.'

c **Argoet**: Argoed is a common place-name. If a region in Powys, it cannot now be identified, and it may even be an alternative name for Powys itself. See also III.45. Stanzas 1 and 2 support the evidence of 'Gwahodd Llywarch i Lanfawr' (EWSP, pp. 414-15) and late antiquarian tradition that Llywarch sought refuge in Powys in his old age, even if Powys is not the setting for Gwên's battle or the original location of his saga.

a'm porthes: There are several possibilities here, probably involving deliberate word-play on the various meanings of *porthi*. The most obvious is that the men of Argoed have long provided support to him as a dependent. In his evocation of his glorious past, *porthi* can mean to support in war. In light of later references to his tiresome garrulity and unpopularity, the sense 'endure, bear, put up with' may also be evoked.

2c **paradwys Gymry**: For the mutation of a proper noun in a genitival relationship with a feminine singular noun see GMW, p. 14, and cf. I.28a above. *Cymry* probably refers to the place, but could also be the people of Wales.

4a **Baglan bren**: *Baglan* is a diminutive of *bagl* from L. *baculus*, perhaps used affectionately since Llywarch is addressing his sole companion. For lenition of a noun in the genitive referring to composition or quality see GMW, p. 14.

kynhayaf: In the four stanzas running through the seasons of the year, Llywarch begins with autumn and ends with spring. It is a poetic commonplace in Classical and early Christian sources to compare the life of man to the seasons of the year, invariably starting with spring. The comparison stresses the brevity of life, as in stanza 14 which implicitly compares the cycle of life to that of a leaf growing and dying in a single year. If there is external influence here, the use of the four seasons is highly original nevertheless. Llywarch is shown to be out of harmony with man and nature in all seasons, and by starting with autumn the series ends with the most striking contrast between the renewal of nature in spring and Llywarch's decline.

6b **Rud cogeu**: Three of the four seasonal verses are further linked at the beginning of line b by a description of a natural feature which at the given season is *rhudd* 'russet, reddish-brown'. This one is perplexing since cuckoos are generally grey and black. Because of this, and some difficulty in the manuscript readings of the second part of line b, various emendations have been suggested; see EWSP, p. 452. Young cuckoos, however, are brown, and this would suit the spring-time reference and unlike some of the suggested emendations preserve the adj. *rud* found in this position in three of the four seasonal stanzas.

goleu ynghwyn: The Red Book reads *goleu ewyn* here, and the two copies of the White Book omit the end of the line. This reading comes from NLW 4973B. The Red Book reading does make sense, 'bright is the foam (of the waves)', and in the two parallel lines of nature description in stanzas 4 and 6 the observations are not connected. The Red Book reading, however, could easily be a corruption of the form which gave the NLW 4973B reading. Several early poems associate spring with the sad cry of the cuckoo, and although the seasonal reference in them is to *cyntefin*, there would be some overlap in the period of cuckoo-call.

c **digarat gan uorwyn**: Another subtle linking involving three of the four seasonal verses is the use of the negative prefix *di-* in line c. *Digarat* is an adjective related to the verb in 4c, and all three lines convey isolation. While *morwyn* is singular, the line has a general force, and can be translated: 'I am rejected by maidens'.

7c The shape of the walking stick's head echoes that of the curly new shoots in line b, but is a symbol of Llywarch's decrepitude rather than renewal. Llywarch's mood does not match that of the season, explaining his grief in observing his walking stick, even though he goes on to address it with comparative warmth in the following two stanzas.

8a **gangen [n]odawc**: The mss. read *ganghen uodawc*, but line c also has *lleueryd uodawc*. It is unlikely that the same word would appear twice in rhyming position. *Bodawg* 'continual' is best with *lleueryd*, referring to the constant speech of the lonely old man; cf. 10c. There are other possibilities for emending the form in line a; see EWSP, p. 543. *Nodawc* 'supporting' would be an otherwise unattested adjective from *nawdd* 'protection, maintenance, support'. If *nodawc* is read here it could also be an otherwise unattested adj. from *gnawd*, cf. *gnawdawl* 'customary'.

9b **I'th elwir**: For *y'th elwir*, possibly a variant of *a'th*, the preverbal particle used to infix the object pronoun.

10 There are 7 stanzas beginning with *Baglan brenn*, the four running through the seasons and 8–10. The order may originally have been 8, 10, 9 since stanzas 8 and 10 have several additional verbal correspondences.

10b **a uo gwell**: Originally, the comparative of the adjective was used predicatively, and this remains a common usage in MW despite the spread of attributive use. The same holds true for a comparative adj. used as an adverb. See GMW, pp. 43 and 229.

The 3rd sg. present subjunctive ending *–o* is more recent than *–wy* (OW *-oe*). The earlier form is not found in the saga *englynion*, but most of the examples of *–o* are not in rhyming position; see IV.13c. See Simon Rodway, 'Two developments in medieval literary Welsh and their implications for dating texts', pp. 71–74.

c **Neut wyf Lywarch**: This type of declaration of the identity of the speaker is found elsewhere in saga poetry. Such statements serve to remind the audience that the poet is speaking in character, and in some instances might have replaced introductory material when identity of the speaker was in itself sufficient for the audience to place the poetry in its story context.

lauar pell: The phrase used as an epithet is lenited, see I.19a above. *Pell* is often used as long in time. The mss. have *lawer*.

11a **Kymwed y mae heneint**: *Kymŵed* is trisyllabic. The mss. all follow the pattern of 12a; the line was emended in CLlH to restore end rhyme which is invariable in an *englyn milwr*. These two incremental stanzas are the only certain instances in the saga *englynion* of the common MW and MnW periphrastic progressive present tense of *bod* + verbal noun; see EWSP, p. 383. *Mae*, originally an interrogative rather than a verb, is also relatively rare; see III.22b and EWSP, p. 369. The rarity of *mae* and the periphrastic construction could be an indication that the bulk of the saga poetry is early. Both the syntax and verbal form, however, may be possible for the proposed period of composition, and the stanzas should not be dismissed lightly as later additions.

From stanza 11 on an uncompromising picture of the infirmities of old age is given, with every stanza except for 15 including the words *hen* or *heneint*.

c **yr ieueinc**: The definite article makes the line a bit long; in the incremental variant in 12c it is omitted before *wraged*. Note the exploitation of the two different plural forms of *dant* for the purpose of varying rhyme.

13a **Dyr gwenn**: Uncertain, in part because the form in the mss. could represent several possibilities in copying from other orthographic systems; see EWSP, pp. 544-45. One of the best solutions, keeping assonance with *gwynn* in the second half of the line, is to see this as representing *dirwyn* 'winding, turning, twisting, eddying'.

b **gne**: While *gne* can be incorporated in a long nominal sentence, 'white is the colour of the edge of the woods/ tips of the trees', i.e. places where snow can settle, it may be best to see this as an interpolation. The rhyme scheme is lavish in this stanza, particularly for a *milwr*, but the internal rhyme of *gne* immediately before the end rhyme is anomalous, and so also is the running on of the second nominal sentence to line b which itself has two nominal sentences. Arranging the verse as an *englyn penfyr* leaves both lines a and b short. Even if something has been lost from line a, *dewr hyd; diwlyd bre* would still be very short and yet appears to be complete. The nature description evokes a winter day which adds to the elderly man's bodily afflictions — in contrast to the lively stag who flourishes in such weather.

14a **Neu's**: The object of the verb is fronted with the infixed object pronoun repeating it in a construction analogous to the *nominativus pendens*.

c **Hi hen**: When the subject of a nominal sentence is a pronoun the order is invariably subject, predicate, a reverse of usual order. As is usual when normal word order is changed the predicate is lenited where relevant (cf. III.76 *hi gyua*).

15a **yssy gas gennyf**: *Bod* + adjective + *gan* expresses an opinion: 'I find it hateful, it is hateful to me'.

b This line can be punctuated and interpreted in two ways. The assonance of *merch* and *march* is best stressed if the line contains a pair of noun + adjective. However, a general love of triads suggests Llywarch is recalling three past pleasures, topped in the following stanzas by four hateful things he now has. This would make *estrawn* a substantive noun rather than an adjective. Normally the conjunction is found between each element in a series, but the syntax of poetry may be looser; cf. 16c below, and a similar line in 'Marwnad Guto'r Glyn' *Meirch a gwyr, merch a garai.*

c **Neut nat**: Generally *neu(d)* introduces a positive statement, and intensifies it to a degree; cf. I.2a. Here *neut* as copula intensifies a *negative* statement.

eu kyuadas: Loosely, 'their [being] suitable/ appropriate'; 'it is not me for whom they are suitable'.

16a **eirmoet**: The compound preposition which consists of preposition plus noun, like *er* + *oed*, is conjugated by use of the possessive pronoun with the nominal element. The third singular form, *eirioed*, eventually replaced all other personal forms, and influence of the third singular can be seen here in even the 1st sg. form in the affection of *er* to *eir* which in the third singular was caused by the m. pronoun. One of the ms. has the original form *er moed*, and those in the White Book tradition have the more modern *eirioet*. See GMW, p. 222. These various forms show how minor changes in copying can change perception of the date of composition.

b **Yt gyueruydynt**: The tense here, imperfect, is best translated as a simple past.

17b **Gwedy gwely keinmic**: This is probably a reference to his former sleeping place in the hall, as opposed to his unvisited bedside of 5c, probably on the fringes of the court. The Medieval Welsh laws specify the sleeping places of some of the chief officers of the court, and earlier sources elsewhere such as *Beowulf* and the early Irish sagas indicate that the hall was the sleeping place for heroic warriors. Note, too, that the lament for Cynddylan's hall states that the ruined hall is now *heb wely*, III.18b. However, *gwely* can refer to the family group which holds ancestral lands which would be a possible sense here although rather broad if Llywarch is referring to the loss of his sons.

c On the metrical pattern of chain *cymeriad* in 17–20 see the Introduction.

tridyblic: The formation is interesting. *Dyblyg* is a borrowing from Latin *duplic-*, but the prefix *dy-* seems to have been understood as the Welsh intensive particle, *dy-*, allowing other numbers to be prefixed to show the number of folds. The logically redundant form, *deuddyblyg*, for instance, is well-attested.

18c **karawd**: This is one of the few examples in the saga *englynion* of the 3rd sg. pret. indicative ending *-awd*. Although common in later Medieval and Modern Welsh, it is innovative. None of the three examples in the saga *englynion* are in rhyming position, as is the case here, so they may either represent outliers of linguistic change or be later substitutions. See Simon Rodway, 'A Datable Development in Medieval Literary Welsh', CMCS 36 (1998), pp. 71–94.

19c **Wi a agheu na'm dygret**: *Kenniret* and *darymret* contain the same root. *Dygret* does not, but there is undoubtedly word-play on the similar sounds and meanings. In the closing verses of the poem there is also play on the idea of desirable things which do not come to Llywarch, or which he cannot frequent, and undesirable things which do come to him. By placing it among those things which do not approach him, it makes Llywarch's expressed longing for death all the more understated and ironic. Compare, too, a similar statement by Heledd in her grief, III.23c *Wi a angheu byrr ym gat*.

20a **hoen**: Metrical uncertainties make the reading here uncertain. *Hoen*, meaning 'joy, gladness', makes good sense, and the pair *hun a hoen* appear elsewhere in poetry. However, *hoen* is a monosyllable which would not rhyme with Gwên and *hen*, and rhyme suspension in the first line of a *milwr* is unlikely. It is possible the long vowels in Gwên and *hen* could form a *proest* rhyme with the diphthong in *hoen*, although this would not conform with later usage. If not, the emendation suggested by Ifor Williams in CLlH, p. 110, may be followed: *ny'm dygret hun na'e ohen* 'neither sleep nor inclination for it comes to me' from *gohen, gwohen*. The similarity to the attested pair *hun a hoen* could have caused a scribe to unconciously substitute.

b **Llawr a Gwen**: Llawr appears in the *Bonedd yr Arwyr* list of Llywarch's sons, and in one antiquarian verse, CLlH I.42c. Even if there was a lost story with verse about him, it is odd to find him singled out here with Gwên whose position in the saga is pre-eminent as the last of Llywarch's sons, and the catalyst to his change of heart. *Llawr* is also a common noun meaning 'champion'. It is possible that *Llawr* in the antiquarian sources is a ghost figure taken from this line misunderstood. If originally written something like **guedi leas laur aguen* which ought to have been understood: *gwedy lleas llawr, a Wen* 'after the death of a champion, o Gwên'. Cf. I.3c.

21 This final stanza is also found at the end of the other poem about Llywarch's lonely old age in the cycle, 'Gwahodd Llywarch i Lanfawr'. Given the tight *cymeriad* of the concluding stanzas, this verse could be a floating verse, or serve as a loose refrain.

a **dynghet a dynget**: There is verbal play here between the form of the noun and verb, and also *figura etymologica*. On concepts of fate in the cycle, see the Introduction. On the phrase and concept, see Thomas Charles-Edwards, '*Mi a dynghaf dynghed* and related problems', in *Hispano-Gallo-Brittonica*, ed. Joseph Eska *et al.* (1995), pp. 1–15.

NOTES 43

III

1 This verse would appear to be separate from the *marwnad* to Cynddylan, since there is framing *cymeriad geiriol* between the opening words of stanza 2 and the closing words of stanza 16 at the end of the *marwnad* proper. Four-line *englynion* are very rare in the saga corpus, although by the eleventh century various forms of four-line *englynion* completely dominate court bardic poetry. One four-line verse is also found at the beginning of *'Englynion Cadwallon'*. In both the Cadwallon poem and Canu Heledd the addition of an extra line may serve to give weight to and set apart a prologue verse. This stanza is an *englyn unodl union*, but there is no rhyme found on the *gwant* as would be found generally in the later bardic instances.

a **Sefwch allan**: The Seithennin poem in the Black Book has a similar dramatic opening: *Seithenhin sawde allan ac edrychuirde*. The phrase *sefyll allan* contains both the notion of rising and going out.

b **Gyndylan werydre**: The order found in the mss. has been reversed for rhyme. The inverted order of modifier, noun is attested in poetry, and as is usual with inverted order lenition occurs. A similar phrase is found elsewhere in stanza 81b *Ffreuer werydre*.

c **Llys Benngwern**: For the lenition of Pengwern see GMW, p. 14. Llys Bengwern is probably the court complex of Cynddylan whose destruction is described in 'Stafell Gynddylan'. A Pengwern in Powys is twice cited in later poetry. Giraldus Cambrensis identified the site as Shrewsbury, an identification which for several reasons is unlikely. Despite other suggestions based on topography and archaeology, the location is unknown. It must lie in the north-east of a larger Powys, including territory now in England. See further, EWSP, pp. 573–74.

d **brotre**: Uncertain. If related to Ir. *brothrach, brothar* 'hair', it could be taken as a longing by youths to have beards, i.e. be old enough to fight to defend their home. Cf. 'Englynion y Clyweit' 69 *gwae ieuangk a eidun heneint* 'woe to the young who desire old age'. Another derivative meaning of Ir. *brothrach* is 'coverlet, blanket, mantle, cloak' which would also make sense here, the burning of the court having deprived the dependant members of even their most basic requirements.

2a **Vn prenn ygwydvit**: This must be taken with the final line of this lament for Cynddylan, 16c *ny elwir coet o vn prenn*. On this framing metrical feature see the Introduction. The usage of *vn prenn* is obviously figurative for Cynddylan. The core meaning of *gwydvit* is wood-hewing, but figuratively it could be taken as 'battle'. Although attested later, *gwyddfid* 'hedge, defensive enclosure' also makes good sense, and can be extended figuratively to 'host, army'. Doubtlessly there is word-play here on the various senses of the words, but it would seem the basic point, made here as a gnomic generalization, is that a single element of a defence — however mighty — cannot withstand too great battle hardship. In 16c there is a variant of this: the mighty warrior cannot in himself provide defence. On the figurative use of a warrior as a tree and an army as a forest in Welsh tradition see further Haycock, *Legendary Poems from the Book of Taliesin*, p. 171.

b **ys**: *Ys*, the absolute form of the copula is used as an impersonal form in MW and at the head of a sentence in mixed order; see GMW, pp. 140–42 and cf. I.8a *yssit*. The usage in the *englynion* is frequently as copula, following earlier usage, see GMW, p. 139, and below 18a, etc.

c **Ac a uynno Duw, derffit**: This proverbial statement is fairly common. *Ac a* is attested as a rare variant of the relative pronoun (GMW, p. 63). This is the form found in the version of the saying in *Breudwyt Ronabwy*, which argues against emending to *ar a* 'that which". See further Richard Glyn Roberts, *Diarhebion Llyfr Coch Hergest*, p. 35.

3a **Kynndylan**: The name of the subject of the *marwnad* is used as part of the opening *cymeriad geiriol* throughout the rest of the poem. This repetition of the name is typical of the saga *marwnadau*, reflecting the intensity of the narrator's grief. It is a feature of Llywarch's *marwnad* for Gwên and the *marwnad* to Mechydd at the end of 'Llym Awel'. The additional verbal patterns here also repay attention. Stanzas 3 and 4 employ the *Kynndylan callon* formula also found in 7–9. However, 3 and 4 compare his spirit to ice and fire, while in the later usage his spirit is compared to that of various ferocious beasts. The series is interrupted by a different opening pattern (with the exception of the initial name), but a verbal pattern concerning the defence of Tren in line c carries the link from 4 to 5 and 6. This sophisticated overlap of verbal *cymeriad* is also a feature in 'Stafell Gynddylan'. The *marwnad* also has a good deal of alliteration on *c* evoking the name of the honorand.

callon: The medieval spelling represents *cal-lon*, not [ɬ]. *Iaen* is disyllabic, rhyming with *benn/ Trenn*.

b **twrch**: The reference in this line is uncertain. *Twrch* 'boar' can be figurative for a warrior, or literally the wild animal. If the latter, the line refers to Cynddylan's peace-time activity of hunting, well-attested for the nobility. It seems more likely, however, that stanzas 4 and 5 refer to Cynddylan's behaviour in battle, paradoxically both icily calm and fiery and impassioned. *Twrch* then would be an enemy warrior, probably Cynddylan's victim. Grammatically *twrch* as the subject and Cynddylan as the victim cannot be ruled out, but in the other stanzas with this opening pattern the references are to Cynddylan and his deeds.

c **Cu a rodeist yr cwrwf Trenn**: The exact significance of this line is also uncertain. Tren is a township or region on the river Tern in Shropshire. (The

English name shows metathesis.) *Cwrwf Trenn* is symbolic of Cynddylan's sovereignty over his land. Although mead is the drink most commonly used in this context (also later in stanzas 69,70), alliteration on the initial letter of the subject, Cynddylan, is heavy throughout the poem. *Cu* must be taken substantively, but it is impossible to be sure what beloved thing Cynddylan sacrificed in his role as ruler. *Rodeist* may be an error for *rodes*, since there is no other direct address to the dead before stanza 13 or 14. Another possibility is that *cu* is an error for *tu* 'side' with an idiom *rhoddi tu* indicating the warrior placed his body in the line of battle.

4a **godeith wannwyn**: The hero's battle ardour is often compared to the rushing fire of a heath burning. The Medieval Welsh laws indicate spring was the usual time for this. For the mutation see GMW, p. 15.

b **o gyflwyn anghyuyeith**: There are several possibilities here, with our ignorance of the background narrative of Cynddylan's fall precluding certainty. Three of the mss. read *anghyfyeith*, but for possible readings based on the Red Book reading *am gyfyeith* 'for one of the same language, fellow countryman' see EWSP, p. 577. 'Giving gifts' seems to have been used ironically for 'fighting'.

c **tref diffeith**: This description obviously refers to the ruined state of Tren after the battle, but there is doubtless a secondary legal meaning to *diffeith* of 'land without an acknowledged owner', in contrast to *Tren, tref y dat* in the following *englyn*. The loss of the rightful rulers and therefore sovereignty is a recurring theme in *Canu Heledd*. Cf. also the discussion of *diua* in 49b and 50a below.

5b **Kadwynawc, kildynnyawc cat**: Here and in 6b it is more likely that the adjectives are being used substantively for Cynddylan, rather than describing his host (with mutation not shown), given the emphasis on the subject of the *marwnad* to the exclusion of all others. The adj. *kyndynyawc* is applied to Cynddylan alone in 8c.

c **tref y dat**: Not merely his father's homestead, but in legal terms his legitimate inheritance, his *treftadaeth*.

6a **ovri**: The adj. *gofri* 'noble, renowned' makes good sense, but *proest* rhyme is rare. It is possible this has replaced *o vru*, with *bru* in a rare sense of 'heart, spirit' providing a link to the *Kynndylan callon* stanzas which frame 5 and 6.

7c **calaned a ledi**: This is a variation of the expression *lladd celain* 'to strike dead'. The variant ending of the 3rd sg. imperfect *ladei* of the mss. has been restored to give obligatory end rhyme; see GMW, p. 121.

8b **buteir ennwir**: The first word is unknown, and the second ambiguous. *Buteir* may be related *bydeir* in 54b, by context possibly a bird of prey; see GPC *buddair*, *byddair*. *Ennwir* can either be a positive adjective < *an* (intensive) + *gwir* 'true', or unfavourable < *an* (neg.) + *gwir*. Since the line undoubtedly refers to Cynddylan, the former is more likely. A possible emendation assuming mistakes in interpreting earlier orthography is *bu terrwyn gynndeiryawc* 'he was ardent and fierce'.

c **kyndynyawc**: See 6b. Stanza 8 interrupts two incremental stanzas, 7 and 9. The correct order should perhaps be 6,8,7,9. Stanza 8 in this position would resume the *Kyndylan callon* pattern but provide a verbal link through *kyndynyawc* with 5 and 6.

10a **gulhwch**: Culhwch is the hero of the earliest Arthurian tale, but virtually unattested outside it. The vast majority of the characters referred to in the saga *englynion* are historical or pseudo-historical. Rachel Bromwich and D. Simon Evans in their edition of the text suggest that Culhwch is a non-traditional character invented for the tale and whose name was substituted later in this stanza for some other name or noun, such as *culwyd* 'lord'; *Culhwch and Olwen: An edition and study of the oldest Arthurian tale*, p. xxix. *Culwydd*, however, is only attested once other than for God. There are numerous overlapping and echoing usages in the *marwnad* which suggest a different solution. Stanza 10 marks the end of three stanzas comparing Cynddylan's spirit (*callon*) to that of various wild beasts, the last of which is a wild boar. The animal imagery in 10 is particularly rich, with line c echoing as well stanzas 3 and 5 at the beginning of the series. Eric Hamp has argued that the first element in *Culhwch* is a substratum synonym for 'pig'; '*Culhwch* the Swine', ZCP 41(1986), pp. 257–58, and Patrick K. Ford has noted further porcine elements in the story which suggest an underlying mythic pig tale of a traditional nature ('A Highly Important Pig'). An archaic common noun meaning 'boar', alliterating with the celebrant, Cynddylan, may be preserved here.

c **twrch**: It is tempting to connect this with 3b; see the note above, although given the extensive animal symbolism the usage need not be the same. The most likely interpretation is that the *twrch* 'boar-like warrior' is Cynddylan who will never return to his patronymy, using a direct object of a verb of motion. If *twrch* is the enemy warrior the line also makes sense, using *adfer* in the sense of 'return, restore', but with no immediate antecedent this interpretation would depend in part on the usage of *twrch* previously in stanza 3.

11 This stanza presents multiple difficulties although the basic sense, that like a true heroic warrior Cynddylan went with equal delight to the feast or the battlefield, is clear. If the unknown *yd adei* is an error for *yd aei* 3rd sg. imperf. of *mynd*, the main sentence would be 'he used to go to battle as to beer'. *Y gallon mor wylat gantaw* would then be parenthetic phrase affirming his high spirits, looking similar to the idiom in 17a and elsewhere except for the conjugated preposition which can perhaps be explained by the fronting of *y gallon*.

12a **borffor wych yt**: The reference is to a splendid garment denoting nobility and rank. *Porffor* might have been used as a substantive noun, but a simple emendation is to *borffor [r]wych yt*; *rwych* 'mantle'. However, the lenition of *porffor* is unexpected and perhaps indicates a feminine sg. noun such as *peis* 'cloak' has been omitted before it. (Stanza 97a alludes to *katpeis Kynndylan.*) Posession in the early period is most often with the dative infixed pronoun with *bod*; cf. I.25a, etc. and below 64a. With nouns the preposition *y*, not *gan*, is found, see EWSP, p. 372. The use of a conjugated rather than infixed pronoun here can be explained by the omission of *bod*.

b **kell esbyt**: This could be figurative for Cynddylan, representing his wealth and generosity. Or, if the first line expresses possession a literal storehouse to provide for guests is another of his lordly possessions.

bywyt ior: *Bywyd*, unlike *buchedd*, is not attested for 'lifestyle, life', although that would make good sense here. The sense 'livelihood, wealth' is attested later, and could also possible here. In CLlH, Ifor Williams suggests emending to *cywyd* 'design, purpose, disposition'. This would give parallel alliteration in the line.

13a **Kyndylan wynn**: *Gwyn* 'fair, fair-haired' is a very common epithet. It is also used with Cynddylan's name in 34c and 47c. Cf. also 'Ffreuer' below. The following observation is addressed to the dead man directly; the *marwnad* follows the usual saga pattern of switching to direct address and second singular forms.

b **Ny mat wisc**: The adjective *mad* can be prefixed to verbs to modify it adverbially, usually commenting on the outcome of the verbal action as fortunate (or unfortunate with the negative). Here, however, it is closer to the basic meaning, 'well'. A similar thought is found in stanza 100a *Ny mat wisc briger nyw dirper o wr yn diruawr gywryssed*. Both *baraf* and *briger* are outward signs of manhood and the status of a warrior. Undoubtedly there is indirect severe criticism of someone in Cynddylan's warband or family in this gnomic statement, a sub-plot of the story of Cynddylan's fall known to the original audience which cannot now be recovered.

c **ny bo gwell**: See II.10b and GMW, pp. 43–44.

14b **armeithyd**: This form is uncertain. It is most likely 2nd sg. pres./fut. of *arfaethu* 'intend, plan' with alternation of *-ei-* and *-ae-* as attested in *cyrraedd*. The internal *-m-* could be explained by failure to modernize earlier orthography or due to the influence of *armäu* with a similar meaning.

c **na bydy[d] lwyt**: The emendation of the 2nd sg. pres./fut. of *bod* to *bydyd* is not strictly necessary, but would be the older form. The expression is a classical one of the true hero sacrificing long life for glory. With this verse there is unambiguously a direct address of the dead to the end of the *marwnad*. There is also a shift to the present tense. In a nightmare of grief Heledd seems to picture and relive Cynddylan's final battle, with stanzas 15 and 16 calling in vain on the dead man to prevent the incursion, ending in 16 with a reprise to the opening picture of a single tree.

15c **Amgeled am vn ny diw**: In these closing stanzas we seem to have Heledd trying to will a different outcome although reality forces its way through. Here she admits her concentration on Cynddylan cannot change events or turn back time.

16a **nenn**: *Nen* is usually 'roof', or figuratively 'chief, lord'. Here the parallel with 15a suggests 'summit, upland'.

c **Ny elwir coet o vn prenn**: This line appears in the medieval proverb lists, but was probably taken from this poem. On the significance, see the note to stanza 2 above.

17 The words *vn prenn* are so distinctive there can be no doubt that they frame the *marwnad* proper. This verse would appear to be out of place, unless the placing of Cynddylan's body on a bier was imagined by Heledd. In 34–44 his body still lies on the battlefield so a better position would be before 'Eglwysau Basa' (45–51) which describes his burial.

18a **Stauell Gyndylan ys tywyll**: On *ys* as copula see above 2b. *Stauell Gyndylan* is fronted throughout (stanzas 18–33). The poem resembles a *marwnad* formally in naming the subject in each verse in a prominent position, as well as in the shift to address in the second singular found in the course of the lament. For the usual order cf. *Ys trist Eu[y]rdyl, Ys moel fy arglwyd*, EWSP, pp. 423, 426.

The form of *stauell* throughout is a relatively rare survival of an OW form without prosthetic *y*, believed to have developed in full after the accent shift. The assonance in this repeated line (and stanza 23) may suggest some sort of prosthetic vowel was intended to be sounded (*ystafell ... ys tywyll*), although the lines would be long if it were counted metrically as a full syllable. For the mutation of the proper noun following a feminine sg. noun see GMW, p. 14.

Stafell, usually 'room, chamber', is best taken as 'hall', the single large one-roomed building which represents the heart of Cynddylan's court. Like the poem in the Urien cycle lamenting the 'hearth' of Rheged, this is sometimes compared to Anglo-Saxon poems concerning the ruined hall; see EWSP, pp. 154–56.

heno: *Heno* is the *gair cyrch* in 11 of the stanzas, and in all but one stanza in the following poems, 'Eryr Eli', 'Eryr Pengwern' and 'Eglwysseu Bassa'. The use of the adverb adds to the immediacy of the lament, but limits poetic opportunity to link the *gair cyrch* to either line a or b. *Heno* or *heddiw* occurs frequently in the saga *englynion* and is also attested (in the OW form *henoid*) in each stanza of the earliest surviving written example of saga type verse, the three Juvencus *englynion*.

The earlier *henoeth* is not precluded in Canu Heledd since none of the examples rhyme.

b **heb wely**: See 'Cân' 17b.

c **wedy**: MnW would use *wedyn* adverbially; for *(g)wedy* as an adverb see GMW, p. 223.

20c **etlit**: The mss. have *elit*.

21a **Stauell Gyndylan ys tywyll y nenn**: The opening line of this stanza, and that of 22, 27, 31, and 33, suggests that the fronting of the subject is separate from the sentence structure, further stressing the subject repeated in the *cymeriad geiriol*. The same holds true for the opening *marwnad* and the following poems about the two eagles, 'Eglwysau Basa' and 'Y Drefwen', although in many instances the fronted words can be taken as a simple subject and translated that way.

c **Gwae ny wna da a'e dyuyd**: The import of this probably gnomic statement is not certain. It is found in the Red Book of Hergest proverb collections, column 1067. It may be a reflection of the helplessness of the non-warrior members of society like Heledd who are not personally able to affect their fortunes. Here the complement of *gwae* is the relative clause which follows 'woe is he who does not….'

22a **heb wed**: The basic meaning of 'without form, shapeless' is suitable for the ruined hall here, but *heb wed* is found for 'unsightly, ugly' which also makes sense.

b **Mae ym bed dy yscwyt**: This is one of the few usages of *mae* in the earlier *englynion*; see EWSP, p. 369, and above II.11–12. The following poems make it clear that Cynddylan is not yet buried. The phrase *ym med* seems to have been used for 'dead' with the poet not alert to the literal connotation.

c **dollglwyt**: This is probably a compound of *toll* (f. of *twll*) 'broken' and *clwyd*, a moveable hurdle used as a closing: 'broken doored'. There is also a figurative meaning of defence which gives a suitable secondary meaning to the line. However, *tollglwyt* does occur in the law texts as a variant of *dorglwyt* 'door-hurdle, door, fig. defence'. The line could be interpreted as in CLlH that given his power there was no need for a door to the hall in the lifetime of Cynddylan, but this is less striking than the picture of destruction leaving the hall open to invasion, and the secondary figurative sense of *dorglwyt* 'defence' would not be appropriate.

23b **Gwedy yr neb**: *Yr* before a consonant here is not an error or remnant of Old Welsh orthography, but a way of indicating elision with *gwedy* = *gwedy'r*. For *y neb* as the antecedent of a relative clause see GMW, pp. 68–70.

pieuat: *Pieu* contains the 3rd sg. pres. indicative of *bod*. Usually it is declined *pi* + the appropriate form of *bod*; *pieuat* is unusual in adding the 3rd sg. imperf. ending to *pieu*.

c **byrr**: Interrogative < *py* 'what, why' + *yr* 'for, because'. It is followed by a preverbal particle, unlike *pyrr* < *py* + *ry*.

24b **hytwyth**: The meaning is uncertain even though *twyth* and compounds of *twyth* are well-attested. The poet seems to be describing a typical position for a fortress, so a meaning such as 'strong, mighty' can be suggested.

c **heb amwyth**: Line b in this poem frequently follows a pattern of listing two things the hall now lacks. The pattern is found in the third line here, varied by the extension to a triad, and in 29c where the two items are modified by a verbal phrase. With only one other uncertain instance of *amwyth* as a noun, this line could be emended on the pattern of 29c by changing to *ai amwyth*, 3rd sg. pret. of *amwyn* 'defend', 'who defended it'. Given the subtle variation in the poem, however, the reading is probably original. *Amwyth* may be a noun 'defence' based on *amwyn*, or a variant of *amnwyth* 'valour, military might'. The line also reads as a linear history: no leader, therefore no host, therefore no defence.

25b **heb gerdeu**: This may possibly refer to the performance of poets if the music was professional. Despite the poets' stress on their role in praise poems they are virtually invisible in the saga *englynion*, with the exception of poems dealing with poets as characters and two references in antiquarian-type single verses. The characters provide their own *marwnadau*, and fame and renown for deeds is not directly linked to praise by poets even by Llywarch except in those two stray verses which are part of the later codification of his many sons.

c **Dygystud deurud dagreu**: This line appears in various proverb lists. The order is poetic: verb object subject.

26c **Hidyl vyn deigyr men yt gynnu**: The line in the mss. is obviously too short; the addition of *vyn deigyr* comes from CLlH, based on the near exclusive use of *hidl* as an adj. describing rain and tears. *Cynnu* is the vn and 3rd sg. pres. indicative of a defective verb 'fall down, descend'. Logically a reference to Heledd's falling tears would be expected, but the singular form of the verb is a problem. It could refer to the hall, half-destroyed and crumbling, but this is strained. Since t̲ can be confused with c̲ in some scripts *men yt* could be an error for *menyc*, i.e. *mynych*, giving good sense: Heledd's tears are abundant and frequently falling; in which case read: *Hidyl vyn deigyr menyc[h] gynnu*.

27b **Heb doet**: *Toet* is apparently < *to* 'roof' with the abstract nominal termination *-ed* or the rare plural ending *-ed*.

c **mu hunan**: The vowel of the accented syllable has affected that of the precdeding unaccented syllable. Influenced perhaps by *minnau, myfi* both *my hunan* and *fy hunan* were found in MW.

28b Gwedy: The use of *gwedy* is elyptical here. It can be expanded 'after (having had) …'.

29b Gwedy y: For a more regular line metrically read *gwedy'r*; cf. 23b. The mss. have *uodawc* for *bodawc*.

c parch a'm buei: See I.8a.

31 Lines b and c are identical in stanza 49.

31c Eluan Powys: The name of a country as an epithet often seems to denote its ruler; cf. *Kyndylan Powys* in 12a above. Elfan is the first of the sons of Cyndrwyn listed in *Bonedd yr Arwyr* (Cynddylan is omitted), and is given the same epithet there. Elfan is named four times in Canu Heledd (28c above; 49c, 99c). His epithet may suggest he ruled before Cynddylan, although the poetry implies he fought with him in the defence of Pengwern. Here and in 49c the epithet may apply to both men.

32b O blant Kyndrwyn[yn]: The line without emendation is short and does not rhyme; the same emendation is made in 47b. The termination *-yn*, *-ing* indicates the descendants of or the line of the person's name to which it is added. The Cyndrwynyn are named in the *awdl* 'Marwnad Cynddylan' l. 49 (ed. EWSP, pp. 174–89) and in Cynddelw's poem 'Gwelygorddau Powys' (CBT, Vol. III, pp. 113–27). The connection with line a is tenuous. In stanzas 28–33 the second line of each stanza except this one begins with *gwedy*. 'After (the death of) the children of the line of Cyndrwyn' would make better sense, but it is difficult to explain the scribal error which would give *o blant* since *o* does not occur in this position elsewhere in the poem. *Tywyll* in line a may have been anticipated from the following stanza, and replace a word such as *amdifad* 'deprived'; 'deprived of the children of the Cyndrwynyn'.

34a Eryr Eli: Eli must be a township or region of Powys on analogy with Eryr Pengwern in the following closely-related poem. It has not been identified with certainty. Both poems describe the feeding on carrion after battle by one of the three traditional battlefield beasts. The second poem has far more incremental repetiton, and is closely linked by verbal echoes to this one. The poet brings to life the horror of Heledd's position, unable to protect her slain brother's body on the battlefield at night. *Heno* is omitted here and in 39a in the mss., but obviously needed for metrics. It is also omitted in 40–42a.

b gwy[a]r llynn: This also occurs as a compound, but this would be less satifying metrically. The mss. have *gwyr*.

35c ygoet: Here and in 36c for the more usual *yg coet* = *yng nghoed*. Possibly OW orthography *icoet* (*yng nghoed*) was misunderstood as *y goed* 'to the woods'.

c trwm hoet ymi: The version in line c of the following stanza has the usual idiomatic use of *bod + ar* for afflictions. The use of both *y* and *ar* in the same expression illustrates the freedom taken in incremental repetition.

37b Dyffrynt Meissir myget: The location is uncertain. Meisir is named as a daughter of Cyndrwyn in the antiquarian stanzas listing Heledd's sisters from NLW 4973B, stanza 109, and in the genealogical tract, *Bonedd yr Arwyr*. The mss. have *mygedawc* which is too long and does not rhyme.

c Dir Brochuael: Cynddelw twice refers to Powys as the country of Brochfael/ Brochfael Ysgithrog, a sixth-century king of Powys; on him see Ifor Williams, PT, pp. xxvii–xxx. The use of this kenning, referring to a ruler not from the Cyndrwynyn, and the reference to long affliction are both anachronistic.

38b Ny threid pyscawt yn ebyr: This line and the previous one suggest the eagle of Eli is an osprey, or white-tailed eagle, sea-eagle, not appropriate for land-locked Powys, but drawing on the traditional imagery of the swooping, fishing eagle (cf. I.20b, and Haycock, *Legendary Poems from the Book of Taliesin*, p. 190.) The eagle could be the subject here, as Ifor Williams notes in CLlH, pp. 210–11, not going to fish because he is feasting on the battlefield. However, with *echediw myr* in line a it seems more likely the poet is presenting a picture of such an efficient predator in his usual feeding haunts that fish do not get past him.

c gwelit o waet: Cf. 43b *ar waet gwyr gwylawt* and 44b *ar waet gwyr gwelit* below. The variation of forms found in the mss. probably indicates some confusion on the part of scribes as to how to modernize an unknown verb. A meaning such as 'feasts' or 'wallows' would suit the context. See EWSP, pp. 590–91 for further suggestions.

40c a gereis: The end of the line is missing but is emended in CLlH on the lines of 42c. Medieval Welsh poetry often features play on different tenses of a verb.

41b euan: This word is uncertain. If *euan* is a genuine form it could have a similar meaning to one of the words in the incremental lines with *aruchel*: *atleis* 'cry' (40) or *adaf* 'claw' (42). See further EWSP, p. 591.

42a penngarn llwyt: *Carn* 'a heap' with *pen* would indicate an arrangement of hair on the top of the head, or in the case of a bird, a tuft of feathers. A bird of prey with a tuft of feathers like a horned owl does not immediately suggest itself. However, Eryr Pengwern, like Eryr Eli, is probably an osprey. The osprey's white head has a dark cap of loose feathers which can be blown upwards to form a tuft.

43a Pell galwawt: (Also 44a *pell gelwit*). *Pell* is both long of time and distance; both suit the context here. It can be an adverb placed before the verb with no preverbal particle following, or, as is more likely, an adverb loosely prefixed to the verb (although mutation is not shown in the orthography). Cf. I.13c.

44c **Ry gelwir Trenn tref lethrit**: This line is parallel to 43c, but for effect a contrast between the splendid town of the past and the present ruin would be expected. This is probably a simple error for *ry gelwit*, imperf. impersonal. *Ry* would act as a perfective particle here, but with the present in 43c it would add a sense of habitual or repeated action; see GMW, p. 168.

45a **Eglwysseu Bassa**: This is probably Baschurch in Shropshire, believed to be derived from an Old English personal name, Bass or Bassa. The place-name would then be anachronistic. However, the plural of *eglwys* does suggest a typical early Celtic ecclesiastical site with numerous small churches and oratories.

c **Argoetwis**: Cf. II.1c. Argoed appears to have been the name of a region of Powys, or perhaps an alternative name for Powys. It is, however, a common place-name.

46a **Eglwysseu Bassa ynt ffaeth**: This is appears to be an example of a *nominativus pendens* construction with the subject fronted and formally set off from the main sentence, rather than of a plural verb used with a plural noun subject; cf. the note to 21a above. *Eglwysseu Bassa* is a grammatically plural place-name and so treated throughout the poem except for 50b where the scribe or poet uses a singular pronoun in referring to the town. The collective must be translated as a singular place-name, cf. the following stanza *Eglwysseu Bassa ynt yng* where the reference is to Cynddylan's grave in the town.

Ffaeth is well-attested but none of the meanings listed in GPC are fully convincing here. For farmland it is 'tilled, crumbling; rich, fruitful', all positive. The burning and blood are perhaps to be understood to have enriched the soil. *Ffaeth*, which gives rhyme on the *gwant*, may have replaced an original *diffeith* used to describe Cynddylan's land in 4c and 83c.

48 The rhyme scheme in this stanza, as well as that of 61, 72, and 108, violates the later rule against *trwm ac ysgafn*, rhyming a long vowel with a short one. Scattered examples in poetry dated before the Poets of the Princes suggests such rhymes were not completely condemned. They would probably have been less jarring after the accent shift.

49b **Gwedy y diua**: The object of *diua* is in line c. The *y* here may be the definite article which can be read as if elided, cf. 23b. But comparing stanza 31, which is identical except for the *y*, suggests it may have been inserted by error by a scribe who thought initially *diua o Loegyrwys* referred to Eglwysau Basa.

52a **Y Drefwenn**: The location of this place-name is uncertain; it may even be a descriptive term, 'the fair/ holy town', for an un-named place. In the works of the poets of the princes Whittington near Oswestry is called Y Drefwen. However, the first element in is from an Old-English personal name Hwita, not 'white'. If

Whittington is intended, the place-name, like Eglwysau Basa, is later than the period in which the poetry is set.

b **eiryoet**: Normally *eirioed* is used with past tenses, and *byth* with present and future, but there are some examples of use of *eirioed* with the present tense, as here. The reference here, too, is both to the present and past.

c **Ar wyneb y gwellt y gwaet**: Blood on grass is an heroic commonplace indicating the ferocious fighting of the warrior, as is blood underfoot (53c); see further Haycock, *Legendary Poems from the Book of Taliesin*, p. 203. For full rhyme, *gwoed*, the older form of *gwaed*, could be read. In 53c, however, *gwaet* seems necessary for internal rhyme; see below.

53b **yglas vyuyr**: This is uncertain. *Myfyr* from Latin *memoria*, used for the special grave of a saint or martyr, is attested in place-names. If, as suggested above *y drefwen* is descriptive rather than a place-name, then Myfyr might be the proper name. *Glas* can be the adjective 'green, verdant', but given the ecclesiastical connotations of *myfyr*, *yglas uyuyr* might be an error for *yglas myuyr* 'the monastic settlement of the *memoria*'.

c **draet**: *Traed* was originally disyllabic and does not appear to have diphthongized before the late OW period. The internal rhyme as well as usage of the Poets of the Princes of the pair *gwaed/ draed* would appear to confirm the plural but with the possible use of earlier *gwoed* in 52c it is just possible the correct reading was originally *dan droed* like English 'under foot' using the singular rather than plural.

54b **y bydeir**: An otherwise unattested word for a bird of prey would make good sense here, as suggested in CLlH, comparing *buteir* in 8b, also uncertain (see above). For possible emendations see EWSP, p. 595.

55a **Trenn a Throdwyd**: In stanza 67 of Canu Heledd it is clear that a second river name acquired an initial *t* to alliterate with Tren. If the same process occurred here the second name would properly be *Rhodwydd*. On *rhodwydd* as a common noun see above I.1c. It may also have been used as a place-name without a further modifier.

b **ysgwyt tonn**: Another heroic commonplace applied to the people of Y Drefwen. No lenition is shown, or else there is provection; see GMW, p. 13.

56a **rwng Trenn a Thraual**: It is uncertain whether *traual* here is a place-name, or as in 55a above a common noun. If a place-name, it should probably be connected with the name of a later court of Powys, Mathrafal. If a common noun, Ifor Williams suggests it is a variant of *tryfal*, perhaps used for a triangular piece of land between a fork in a river.

57a **Gwynn y byt**: For the modification of a noun by an adj. followed by a possessive pronoun referring to the noun modified by the adjectival phrase, here Ffreuer, see GMW, p. 37. The phrase is a stereotyped exclamation.

Freuer: One of Heledd's sisters, also mentioned in 81 where the land seen from the Wrekin is called *ffreuer werydre*. She is found in the antiquarian stanzas listing the daughters of Cyndrwyn (below 108), and in the *Bonedd yr Arwyr* list of the children of Cyndrwyn.

mor yw diheint heno: This is open to ambiguity, depending on the interpretation of *diheint*. On analogy with 58a, however, it would seem this description applies to Heledd, not Ffreuer. The equative form is used here in exclamatory fashion; the order *mor* + *bod* + adj. is well-attested in early poetry. Translate: 'how painful it is'.

c **yt lesseint**: See I.28b. The line is rather long; the preverbal particle could be omitted.

58a **mor yw gwann**: The exclamatory construction requires the more unusual meaning of *gwan* as 'sad, depressing'. Heledd later describes herself in the poem as *gwanglaf* (62) where both 'weak' and 'sad' would be possible.

c **eryr**: *Eryr* is used figuratively here as 'hero, leader'.

b **am damorth brodyrde**: Cf. also III.81c *hiraeth am damorth vrodyrde*. These are the only two instances of *damorth* which is uncertain in meaning. 'Slaughter, death' or 'conquering' would make sense from the context in both cases. *Brodyrde* is also rare and uncertain. Possibly it is a compound of *brodyr* with the adj. *de* 'burning, ardent, passionate' which gives good sense.

c **Duhunaf**: On the form see I.12c.

61c **coch dagreu**: This is almost certainly a reference to tears of blood believed to be shed in situations of extreme grief in many cultures. The mss. have *chocheu* for *coch*, probably repeating the ending of *dagreu* in error.

62b **yn wanglaf**: The usage of *yn* + adj. is not found in the copula sentence in early poetry, but is attested after a pronoun; see T. Arwyn Watkins, 'The Descriptive Predicative in Old and Middle Welsh', p. 289. The line would be a better length without it, however. The mss. have a wide range of minims which could be misreadings of *yn*: *ny, uy, wy, ni*.

63b **Ny hannoedynt o'r diffaeth**: Here *diffaeth* must be taken as a pl. substantive noun.

c **wyr**: This is probably lenited because it is in apposition to *brodyr* in line a, and the unexpressed pronominal subject of *hanoedynt*.

64b **gywrenin llu**: Either the mss. do not show lenition, or the final /n/ of *gywrenin* has caused provection of lenited /l/; see GMW, p. 20.

c **Ny echyuydei ffyd ganthu**: Before a vowel the expected form of the negative preverb would be *nyt*, but there are a few exceptions to this to be found in OW and MW. *Echyuydei* is probably an error for *echuydei* 3rd sg. imperfect indicative of a verb **echfod* 'to be wanting, to ebb.' *Ffyd* generally is found in religious contexts and so does not make a good deal of sense here. Perhaps it has been substituted for *cret* which had secular meanings such as 'oath, promise, fidelity'; i.e. they kept their pledges made before battle.

65a **Medlan**: Another daughter of Cyndrwyn. She is also named in the antiquarian verses listing Cyndrwyn's daughters, below 108. See there for the discussion of possibly sovereignty elements in their names.

66a **vch**: All three rhyme words in this stanza lack the glide vowel after *u* found in later Middle Welsh before ch.

b **nyt eidigafaf y dwyn vy buch**: Literally 'I will not tolerate the bearing/carrying off? of my cow'. The sense here with the concessive clause in line a is far from clear, not helped by the wide range of meanings of *dwyn*. Perhaps there is some sort of word play on *uchel* as both high and noble and the possibility of loss of the cow on the rugged terrain. Since the line is rather long even omitting the suffixed 1st sg. pronoun emendation can be considered. If *af* were repeated and the suffixed pronoun then added *eidigaf* could be the 3rd sg. pres./fut. indicative: 'It does not tolerate bearing my cow'. The stanza would seem to reflect Heledd's dire change of circumstances like 69–72.

c **ys ysgawn gan rei vy ruch**: *Gan* here denotes an opinion. 'Some consider my mantle light' is perhaps figurative for belittling her burden in life.

Stanzas 67–68 are omitted

69b **gelyn**: The mss. have *gelein, galein*. This is probably an error in modernizing OW *e* as *ei* rather than *y*. *Kelyngar* in 70b confirms the emendation made in CLlH.

c **Ry'm goruc y uedw**: Manuscript variants have *yn uedw*. Both a direct object and constructions with *yn* are attested after *gwneuthur*. Comparing 60a, *a'm gwna heint*, *y* is best taken as the suffixed 1st sg. pronoun. This poem has many connections with the possible role of Heledd as sovereignty goddess: her changed appearance and circumstances need no supernatural explanation, but her drunkenness, specifically on the mead of the regions of Bryn and Tren, recall the association of the goddess with drink.

71a,b **o dymyr Hafren/ Y am dwylan Dwyryw**: This is the only mention of the Severn river in the cycle, casting further doubt on the view that Pengwern was the Welsh name for Shrewsbury. Dwyryw could refer to the two branches of the river Rhiw which meet the Severn near Garthmyl.

c **vy mot yn vyw**: The usage of the vn *bod* for subordinate clauses is not well attested in early poetry; cf. I.2c. This could be an early example, 'woe's me ... that I am alive', but could also be interpreted as 'woe's me ... for my being alive'.

72b [**mawr**]: The line is short. *Mawr* is the suggested addition in CLlH.

Stanzas 73–75 are omitted here.

76 After 65 the temporal tightness of the first section is broken. Poems tend to be shorter, and there are brief epigrammatical verses like this one and the next, as well as some material which may not have originally belonged to the cycle. Nevertheless, 'Gyrthmyl' also evokes succinctly the idea of the sovereignty goddess mourning for her people: *if* the place were a woman she would be weak and lamenting — like Heledd herself. The location and name of Gyrthmwl are both uncertain. It is perhaps a corruption of Garthmyl on the Severn.

c **Hi gyfa**: For this construction see II.14c. Here the reversal of the usual order of a nominal sentence when the subject is a pronoun causes the lenition of the predicate.

77a **Ercal**: *Erchal* would be the expected form. Possibly the scribes failed to modernize Old Welsh orthography rc for rch, but more likely there is influence of the Shropshire place-names with the element Ercall, which may be English in origin and therefore anachronistic.

b **Moryal**: This is an attested personal name, but there is no evidence of connection with the family of Cyndrwyn.

c This is a common topos in laments. The prefix *ry* clearly gives a perfective meaning to the present tense verbs here.

78a **Heled hwyedic**: This is the first indication of the narrator in the cycle, in a straightforward, unambiguous way of self-naming, and also as part of a dialogue with vocative naming, both common ways of ensuring a poem or cycle in character would be correctly identified. There is evidence elsewhere for knowledge of Heledd: she is listed in the *Bonedd yr Arwyr* list of Cyndrwyn's children, appears in the triads along with Llywarch, and is given a verse in 'Englynion y Clyweit'. However, as a female figure of misfortune it is to be expected that she was not frequently evoked by the bardic poets. The name Heledd appears to be unique to the saga figure. It is uncertain whether it is connected with the the common noun *heledd* 'salt pit'. On Heledd in medieval and modern literature and scholarship see further Marged Haycock, 'Hanes

Heledd hyd yma', *Gweledigaethau: Cyfrol Deyrnged yr Athro Gwyn Thomas*, J. W. Davies, ed. (Abertawe, 2007), pp. 29–60.

The epithet, *hwyedic*, is unfortunately not clear. In the triads she is one of the three *anuodawc* 'homeless, wandering'. Something similar would be suitable here, and in EWSP it is suggested this could be a corruption of **chwifiedig/hwifiedig* from *chwifiad* meaning 'wandering'. In this final section we see Heledd travelling around Powys having lost her home.

b **yt**: The mss. have *yth* here and in 79b.

c **bro[dyr]**: The mss. have *bro*; the emendation is from CLlH and required for sense with *eu tir*.

79a **Heled hwyedic a'm kyueirch**: The opening suggests Heledd's questions are addressed to another speaker, although Heledd's question in 78 may be a *cri de coeur* addressed to God. Emending *a'm* to *a'th* would make both verses cries to God, but it is difficult to see how the error would have occurred.

80a **ar dirion dir**: While the usual sense of *tirion* 'gentle' is acceptable here, the more uncommon 'fallow, uncultivated' is better, and recalls the concerns about the disruption to the cultivation of the land explored in 'Eglwysau Basa' and 'Y Dref Wen'.

b **O Orsed Orwynnyon**: Verses 73–74 omitted here celebrate the deeds of a certain Gorwynnion who kept the cattle of Edeirniawn, a commote in Powys, safe from rievers. The place-name here may have led to their inclusion, since elsewhere Gorwynnion is listed as one of Llywarch Hen's sons. The *gorsedd* could refer to a grave mound associated with a hero as in 'Englynion y Beddau', but the term is also used for a look-out site.

81a **[olygon]**: From CLlH. The line is short in the mss.

Dinlleu Ureconn: The mss. show a good deal of confusion over the form of this name. *Dinlle* found in one gives rhyme on the *gwant*, but the other examples point to *Dinlleu*, like the original form of the place-name in Arfon. *Ureconn* must be connected with the Wrekin, the prominent hill which gave its name to the district. The Roman name for Wroxeter, *Viriconium*, is *Cair Guricon* in the *Historia Brittonum*. The form here has either been corrupted in copying or influenced by English 'Wrekin'.

b **Ffreuer werydre**: Cf. the opening stanza, which speaks of gazing on '*Gyndylan werydre*'. This cannot be called Ffreuer's land with the same political meaning as the earlier usage, again suggesting Heledd and her sisters have taken on aspects of the sovereignty goddess.

c **damorth vrodyrde**: Cf. 59b above.

A fragmentary stanza is omitted here

83a **Kynan, Kynndylan, Kynnwreith**: *Kynan* may be an error for Cynon son of Cyndrwyn named in 32c. The *Bonedd yr Arwyr* list of Cyndrwyn's children, however, gives both names, as well as Cynwreith, named with Cynddylan in a stray stanza, 110; see EWSP, p. 444.

c **tref diffeith**: See 4c above on the possible legal connotations.

84b The statement that the hero did not yield a foot of ground in battle in a typical heroic one.

85a **ny vall**: Uncertain. *Ny* rather than *nyt* suggests *vall* is a verb, but likely forms do not make good sense, and a 3rd plural would be more likely. In rare cases *ny* is found for the negative of the copula rather than *nyt*. *Gwall* then gives good sense, and a *proest* rhyme: 'it was not lack'.

b **coll**: Haycock, *Legendary Poems from the Book of Taliesin*, pp. 212–23, notes that the comparison of her brother to hazel rods gains resonance through the homynyn *coll* 'loss'.

86c **yr ffuc**: 'falsely, by deception'.

87b This line illustrates the difference between the absolute and conjunct forms in the 3rd sg. present indicative, as do many early proverbs. See GMW, p. 118–19 and the note to I.7b.

c **[Tru] ar a**: For the demonstrative pronoun *ar* as antecedent to a relative clause see GMW, p. 70. The addition of *tru* is from CLlH. With no direct evidence another expression of dismay may have been omitted here.

Three stanzas, 88–90, are omitted here. Two celebrate a certain Hedyn and one speaks of a boar's lair. They are of uncertain relevance to Canu Heledd although the casting of shame on the manhood of those who let down Hedyn and the probable figurative use of the boar as an enemy warrior provide links to earlier material.

91 This poem about Caranfael bears an uncertain relationship to the main cycle of Canu Heledd. As discussed below, there may be more than one speaker. If there is only one Heledd is not a likely narrator. The statement that Caranfael literally and figuratively inherited the mantle of his father, Cynddylan, also contradicts the statements which suggest Heledd has lost all her family, and that there is no hope for a valid successor in Powys after the death of Cynddylan. The poem follows the conventions of a saga *marwnad*, with the name of the hero in every stanza after the first. It is also striking for the many conventions of praise for the warrior and ruler.

91a **Ny [wn y] ae nywl ae mwc**: The opening makes use of the *topos* that warriors fighting fiercely raise battle dust obscuring the field. There is also the saga device of 'alternative explanations' discussed by Patrick Sims-Williams along with parallels from Irish and Old English, BBCS 27 (1978), pp. 505-14. Here the speaker runs through the possible reasons for obscured sight, before stating it is due to savage fighting. For the use of *ae ... ae* see GMW, p. 175.

The emendation is from CLlH and justified by the minims in the mss. reading of *ny wy* if from *ni un* misread and modernized.

c **Ygweirglawd aer**: This line must be considered with 92a. In 92a *y weirglawd aer* suggests that *y* is the definite article, but a suffixed 1st sg. pronoun after the verb *edeweis* is also a possible reading. In 91 nasal mutation of *yn + g* is possible, although the preposition *ar* would be more natural. In which case read *y gweirglawd* and assume lenition was not shown because it was initially interpreted as a nasal mutation.

92a **Edeweis y weirglawd aer**: This line forms the crux of the interpretation. Ifor Williams suggests this verse belongs to a follower of Caranfael who has returned to report his death to Heledd who then mourns him. The following stanzas resemble a saga *marwnad* although Caranfael's death is not made explicit. However, a single verse by a second speaker would be unusual in the cycle. It could be avoided by reading *Endeweis* 'I have heard', a variant on the typical *gweleis* formula of witnessing greatness used here in reference to the obscurity of vision caused by the amount of war dust raised? Either way, as noted above Heledd may not be the narrator and the poem may belong to a separate saga tradition in which Caranfael fought on after Cynddylan's death.

c **Garanmael**: This form appears to partially preserve an OW spelling for Caranfael. Caranfael may actually have been Cynddylan's cousin rather than his son; see Jenny Rowland, 'The Family of Cyndrwyn and Cynddylan', BBCS 29 (1981), pp. 526-27.

93a **kymwy arnat**: This is another instance of *ar* being employed to denote affliction, disease, sorrow, etc. *Cymwy* can also be used for battle, one of several words meaning stress, work, hardship, etc. which extend to this sense; cf. *kymwyat* in 14a. A similar development can be seen in *kyniuiat* in line c, from *cynifio* 'labour, strive'.

94a **Kymwed ognaw**: This is similar to the description of the warriors of the *Gododdin* being *chwerthin ognaw*. *Cymŵedd* is trisyllabic.

c **Dywedwr**: An orthographic error for *diwedwr < diwedd + gŵr*, the warrior who guards the rear in retreat, or the last to retreat, not the last of the Cyndrwynin. This stanza with its series of heroic epithets resembles the style of praise poetry.

95a **[dihat]**: A word has been omitted in all the copies. *Dihat* fits in a series of adjectives beginning with *dih-*. *Dihadu* 'deprive of offspring (seed), disinherit' is attested rather late, although 'disinherited' suits the context. *Di* (neg) + *had* 'without seed, without descendants' would also leave a man more dependent on a strong, just ruler.

b **diholedic**: A variant of *deoledig*, maintaining the assonance.

c **ynat**: *Ynad* here probably has more the sense of a ruler rather than judge, although it may evoke the role of the ruler upholding legal rights. Stanza 96 suggests that for some reason Caranfael rejected the role, or perhaps was killed in battle before ruling.

97a **gatpeis Gynndylan**: One proverb in the Red Book list states: 'everyone goes to battle in his father's cloak', the literal probably encompassing the figurative as here.

c **Ffranc**: This rare word occurs in the three Juvencus *englynion* where the consensus is that the word for a man of the continental Franks became a synonym for mercenary, although 'freed man' from *francus* is also possible. Here *Ffranc* may be a Germanic-speaking warrior; see Jenny Rowland, 'Old Welsh *franc*: An Old English borrowing?', CMCS 26 (1993): 21–25.

The brandishing of a spear followed by a verbal challenge is highly stereotyped in heroic literature, suggesting this line refers to Caranfael promising battle, whether to his mercenary followers or Germanic enemies.

98 Unlike the previous poem, this poem about Heledd and an un-named sickly brother almost certainly belongs to the cycle. It is a reminder that all the details of the story of Cynddylan's downfall are not recoverable from the poetry. 100a echoes the complaint in stanza 13 that a man should not outwardly display the marks of a warrior who does not behave as such. This dialogue perhaps shows Heledd rebuking one of her brothers whom she blames for not living up to her other brothers's deeds. As in the case of Llywarch, the goading to war by a non-combatant, in this case a woman, would be contrary to heroic expectations. The excuse of illness offered by Heledd's adversary here would make her criticism distasteful, but the final verse suggests the man may indeed have shirked the harsh realities of war. Ifor Williams took this poem along with statements about Heledd's tongue causing her misfortune to hypothesize that Heledd goaded Cynddylan and her brothers unwisely, like Llywarch. This poem suggests there was no such need, and that one brother only was reluctant.

b **ny dyrchafwn vy mordwyt**: This custom is better attested in early Irish literature. It appears to be similar to touching the brim of a hat rather than removing it entirely — a mark of respect which conveys the intent by a partial gesture. In this case, it would replace rising to greet an equal or superior, although the Irish evidence suggests the gesture was used for equals and full standing for superiors.

c a gwynei claf gornwyt: Lack of knowledge of the underlying story is a problem here. *Claf gornwyt* would appear to be a vocative address here, with the brother complaining or suffering from an illness. *Cornwyd* 'boil, abscess' is associated with leprosy, as is *claf* used as a noun, although it can also be simply a sick person. Heledd's lack of sympathy for her suffering brother might be explained if the illness is leprosy, commonly believed to be a punishment for sin. His failure in battle may have predated his illness in that case, if not completely feigned or over-emphasized (101).

99a Brodyr a'm bwyat inneu: This looks like a response to a statement by Heledd about her brothers, cf. stanzas 85 and 86 and in 104–06. Rearranging the stanzas to give Heledd's two verses followed by the sick brother's two gives a logical order to both claiming kinship to the glorious brothers.

b Ny's cwynei gleuyt: The infixed object pronoun supports taking *cwyno* here as 'suffer from, be ailing' rather than 'complain of' with the illness the subject. Heledd speaks of complaining of illness, and the brother of suffering from it.

100a Ny mat wisc briger: Cf. 13 *ny mat wisc baraf*. *Briger* is long hair, also associated with being a warrior.

b o wr: 'from (being a) warrior'.

c leuawr: For lenition of the predicate after the verb 'to be' see GMW, p. 20. *Llefawr* 'crying, wailing' may be translated something like 'my brothers weren't crybabies', the antithesis of the warrior ethos.

broder: The alternative pl. form is used for rhyme in this stanza. Line b has a generic rhyme.

Two stanzas concerning the graves of heroes are omitted here.

104a Pedwarpwnn: The term seems to single out four of Heledd's brothers as special rulers. *Pwnn* is uncertain, perhaps 'chieftain, leader, lord'.

b Ac y bob un penn teulu: This line can be variously interpreted: '*Ac i bob unben deulu*', '*i bob un pen deulu*' or '*i bob un benteulu*'. 105b suggests '*i bob un*' is the correct division. If each lord (*penn*) had a host, it would follow that the host would have a *penteulu* 'chief officer of the warband', so the second reading is followed here, but the first would have the same meaning although less supported by the orthography. Four brothers, then, were powerful enough to control personal warbands.

c y du: Uncertain. The parallel lines contain an adjective, conveying the loss of rightful and just rulership.

105b Ac y bop un gorwyf nwyvant: Both *gorwyf* and *nwyvant* could be present tense verbs, but this gives little sense. *Gorwyf* is attested, and is perhaps from *go* and *rhwyf* 'pride, arrogance'. Like a host, a steed is a necessity for a leader, so could this be an error for or a variant of *gorwydd*? With *Nwyfiant/ nwyfant* 'passion, vigour' this would give: 'and to each one a steed of vigour'.

107 Seven additional stanzas are found only in the copy in NLW 4973B, including these antiquarian verses listing Heledd's sisters which echo the pattern in which Heledd evokes her brothers. The nine sisters are grouped in the same sets of three in the *Bonedd yr Arwyr* list although not in the same order. Only four sisters are named in the main body of poetry, Heledd, Meddlan, Ffreuer, and Meisir. Nevertheless, some of the extra names are interesting for their possible connection with sovereignty themes.

107a **Amser y buant addfwyn**: Cf. 98a.

c **Gwladus**: The name is not uncommon. It has an obvious derivation from *gwlad* 'land', as does Gwledyr in 109c.

108c **Medwyl a Medlan**: Both names probably have *medd* as the first element, most likely *medd* 'mead', linking them with the sovereignty drink. Meddwyl may be from *medd* + *hwyl* 'pleasure'. Meddlan rhymes here with *-an* but with *-ann* in stanza 65. There seem to be the occasional violation of the later bardic rule against *trwm ac ysgafn* (light vs heavy syllables) in early verse; see 48 above. This composition may be later and antiquarian, however.

There are four additional stanzas in NLW 4973B only. One resembles earlier stanzas about Tren. There are two stanzas to Llemenig mab Mawan and an important stanza linking Cynddylan to the battle of Maes Cogwy. These last three are probably not related to Canu Heledd.

IV

The orthography of the White Book and Red Book is far more familiar to students of Middle Welsh than that of the Black Book of Carmarthen, the sole manuscript for 'Llym Awel'. For this reason a partially modernized version of the first ten stanzas has been appended to the text to aid familiarization with the spelling system. A useful description of the main points of this spelling system can be found in Nicolas Jacobs, *Early Welsh Gnomic and Nature Poetry*, pp. xxxiii–iv and a detailed analysis by Paul Russell, 'Scribal (In)consistency in Thirteenth-century South Wales: The Orthography of the Black Book of Carmarthen', SC 43 (2009), pp. 135–74. A further motivation for getting acquainted with this type of orthography is that it occasionally appears in Red Book/White Book texts, or may lie behind errors which justify emedation. Russell's work also shows just how difficult it is to detect forms or spellings which are only dateable to the Old Welsh period.

The main features of this orthography are as follows:

u, v, w are all used for both u and w as vowels
v, w, u are all used for v as a consonant, with w favoured in final position
f, ff are both used for ff; but *ff* occasionally can be used for v
i is used both for i and y; y can be used for both y or i
t in final and medial position is normally used for /ð/
d in final and medial position is normally /d/

1a Llym awel: See I.2b. The winter description relies heavily on nominal sentences and the 3rd sg. absolute ending. This opening line has three parts facilitated by the short nominal sentences although three part lines are generally rare; cf. stanza 17. The rhyme pattern in this *penfyr* verse is also unusual, with the *gwant* coming very early and copious rhyme in line b with the *gair cyrch*.

b On the 3rd sg. pres./fut. absolute ending which is frequent in gnomic and nature description see the note to I.7b. It is used extensively in this poem. In similar gnomic verse it tends towards conveying a sense of the usual or customary.

c **ry seiw gur ar vn conin**: The preverbal particle *ry* is most associated with adding a perfective sense to the verb, but here it is a sense of possibility which is conveyed. The line seems to have a link to riddling. A merely frozen stalk would be too brittle to support a person. The references to lakes, ponds and ice in the winter descriptions suggest that the single stalk is under clear ice which does the real supporting. Possibly the description of Sgilti Yscawndroed who is described in *Culhwch ac Olwen* as able to walk on stalks without bending a single one is also evoked ironically.

2b goruchel guaetev: The loud cries are clearly the wailing noise of wind.

rac bron banev bre: The compound preposition *rhag bron* 'in front of' generally has the sense of 'in the presence of (a person)' so it is best to take *bron* with *banev*.

c **breit allan orseuir**: Cf. 21e *breit guir orseuir allan*. With the verb *gorsefyll*: 'scarcely does one linger outside' or 'endure outside'. Here the adverb *allan* separates the prefixed adverb *breit* from its verb; in 21e it is the interjection *gwir*. Lenition is a normal indicator that regular syntax has been broken. Given the high wind the sense 'stand up outside' might be possible.

3 This stanza is irregular metrically. The reasons for the emendation are discussed in EWSP, p. 632, as well as other possibilities.

c **coed in i bluch**: The sense is clearer than the precise syntax. While it is satisfying to arrive at an acceptable translation, it is also possible to learn much about interpreting Medieval Welsh from exploring the various possibilities. *Coed* is 'forest, woods'. The usage for 'wood, firewood' appears to be late. Kenneth Jackson in his edition, *Early Welsh Gnomic Poems*, took this later sense with the n. *blwch* meaning 'box', *coed im bluch*, taking the ms. *ini* as an error for *im*. It gives a rather cosy picture of firewood stashed by the fire which is not in keeping with the rest of the description stressing bitter weather outdoors. Much better meaning came from comparison with the Breton adj. *blouc'h* 'bare', attested in the name of one of the early Welsh poets listed in the 9thc. *Historia Brittonum*, Blwchfardd, a 'bare, beardless or bald' poet. (There may be an implied contrast in the poem with the bearded stalks of 4b.) Uncertainties remain which have already arisen in the discussion above: 1. the meanings of words, and how early evolved meanings came into being, 2. the uncertainties of ms. readings of minims, that is simple strokes forming the letters *i*, *n*, *m*, *u*, *v* and by extension the orthographic variants which could be represented by these letters, 3. the syntax of the line and any grammatical mutations which may or may not have been represented in the orthography or which could have been incorrectly interpreted.

If the collective usage 'trees' is sufficiently early the phrase can be taken *yn eu blwch*, 'in their (state of being) bare', i.e. 'trees are bare'; otherwise take *coed* as 'forest' (3rd sg. m.), *yn ei flwch*, with mutation not shown as is fairly common. It has been suggested *i ni* is an error for *im*, giving a rare example of the predicative *yn* being followed by the nasal mutation of *bluch*. But not only is the mutation rare, the predicative *yn* + adj. is is not attested in early saga poems as opposed to usage of copula constructions. It could be argued that this construction was used here to facilitate rhyme, but if that is the case it is odd that it does not occur more frequently. The pleasure of reading the poems in the original does not require all this analysis, but such attention will help to indicate how certain an interpretation is and increase linguistic skills.

5a **Ottid eiry**: MW *eira* is disyllabic, but the *y* in *eiry* represents a semivowel from an earlier monosyllabic word ending in –*g*. The earlier poets usually treated such words as monosyllabic, but that does not give completely regular metre in all of the stanzas here. Possibly poets or performers in a transitional period could exploit both forms as required metrically, or not all of the descriptive verses are of the same date.

b **o'e neges**: On *o'e* see I.26c above.

6b **segur yscuid ar iscuit hen**: The gnomic statements concerning warriors in the poem appear to be inconsistent, encouraging the interpretation that the first section, like 22–29, is a dialogue. Since the opening stanzas lack a clear pattern of speakers and point of view I have suggested they represent an internal debate of a single speaker who has been invited by Pelis (addressed in the clear dialogue section) to take part on a dangerous wintertime expedition. The speaker weighs his reasonable objections and observations on the harsh weather with gnomes that put the other side of the question: concern that he might be mistaking wise caution with cowardice (10c, 15c), and gnomes suggesting the outcome should be left not to debate but fate tempered by experience (13c, 20c). The statement here suggests the hero may be rather old for such an expedition, and so excused, but is contrasted in 7c with the glory that is the brave warrior armed for battle which part of him longs for. This interpretation assumes stanzas like 8 and 19 to be intrusive, attracted because of the theme, as well as some of the stanzas with nature description. (Most of the descriptions of winter weather and landscape do serve to back up the speaker's reluctance and questioning of the wisdom of the expedition.) The gnomic poems in *englyn* metres use many of the saga techniques to unify very disparate material. The high proportion of nature description and gnomes in 'Llym Awel' may have led to less textual stability, particularly if the saga story context had been forgotten.

7a **reo**: This preserves an Old Welsh spelling for *rhew*.

b **gosgupid**: The absolute ending would not originally have been used with a verb having a preverb as here. Generally speaking the absolute is used correctly and consistently in saga verse. For a discussion of the usage by the Poets of the Princes, see Simon Rodway, 'Absolute forms in the poetry of the Gogynfeirdd: functionally obsolete archaisms or working system?', *Journal of Celtic Linguistics* 7 (1998), pp. 63-84, and more recently *Dating Medieval Welsh Literature*, pp. 85-116.

8b **diuryssint vy keduir y cad**: This verse is found elsewhere in the Black Book in the collection of verses about Llywarch Hen's sons, but without the pronoun *vy*, a reading better for sense and metre. Compare 'Marwnad Gwên' sts. 20 and 21 for the stereotyped picture of the excluded former warrior watching warriors depart for battle. Much closer in wording, but with a springtime setting more appropriate to military campaigning, are verses 17 and 18 of 'Claf Abercuawg'; cf. 17:

> Kynneuin kein pob amat
> pan vryssyant ketwyr y gat
> mi nyt af anaf nym gat.

('Early summer — every growth is fair. When warriors hasten to battle I do not go; an affliction does not permit me'.) This 'floating verse' which exists in several variants appears to be an example of the poem attracting extraneous material (see above 6b). If the speaker has been asked to join a dangerous expedition it would be unlikely that he would be prevented by disability or lasting injury (*anaf*), or already be witnessing warriors rushing to battle. Allowing that this verse and others may be intrusive certainly aids interpreting the poem, but to avoid special pleading the possibility or probability will be noted here without excluding them outright.

10c **meccid llvwyr llauer kyghor**: This human gnome should probably be interpreted that the coward generates many arguments to support his reluctance to go to battle, but it is possible to interpret it as the coward encourages many points of view in discussion to avoid the issue being settled. The former would be better with the notion of the internal debate of the narrator who is scrupulously examining his motivation.

11a **Eurtirn**: This is a compound of *eur* 'golden, ornamental, fine' with *dwrn*, pl. *dyrn* from the basic meaning 'fist, hand'. Of the definitions in GPC only 'handle' appears to make sense with drinking vessels. Drinking horns, however, do not appear to have had handles since the shape of the horn itself makes it easily held. There is archaeological and textual evidence for ornamental bands around the rim (cf. I.11b on a war horn), and sometimes an elaborate terminal mount ending in a knob or zoomorphic figure; cf. the depiction of a mounted Pictish warrior drinking from a horn from Invergowrie. Perhaps it is this mount which is meant here since *dwrn* was also used for 'sword hilt, pommel, knob' etc.

cluir: *Clwyr* has a wide range of meanings, many of which could with ingenuity be made to fit here. If the pl. of *cloer* 'coffer' there could be a reference to a piece of furniture on which drinking horns are arrayed, but the more likely picture would be of winter feasting with the horns in use, taking *clwyr* as 'host, troop'. Most of the description focuses on bad weather and difficulty of travel rather than on the opposing comforts of staying indoors.

12b **Dit diulith**: Stating the day is *di-wlith* 'without dew' makes little sense given the winter weather. This is probably an example of *th* for /ð/; cf. *divlit* 14c below.

The second half of this line is missing. There is insufficient evidence to attempt a reconstruction.

c The prediction of bad weather from red skies in the morning is ancient and widespread, with a basis in actual observation.

13b **Reuid rev pan vo**: Line a speaks of the cold covering on the ford. This line seems to be saying ice will form when conditions are suitable.

c **Ir neb goleith lleith dyppo**: This gnome matches the unstoppable force of nature forming ice and presents a note of fatalism. The debate on the wisdom of expedition ultimately may be irrelevant since death cannot be avoided simply by caution. It also suggests the narrator may be worried as in 10c that he is being evasive in a cowardly fashion by considering the weather dangers.

The 3rd sg. subjunctive endings are later, and appear to rhyme with *godo* and *agdo* in line a. See above II.10b.

15b **Glas cunlleit**: *Cunlleit* is uncertain. GPC under *cunllaith, cunllaidd* suggests it is 'fresh grass or herbage', but given the winter conditions green growth is unlikely. Perhaps *glas* has been misplaced from the next stanza and a more appropriate adj. such as *crin* (cf. 14b) should be restored. For further suggestions see EWSP, p. 634.

c **Dricweuet llyvrder ar gur**: Another general human gnome deploring cowardice in a warrior.

16 Verses 16 and 17 end with contrastive weather predictions, but form a close pair in their pattern, particularly the less common 3-part opening lines. 18 immediately contradicts 17 (*hinon uit/ Driccin imynit.*) They could be relevant to the internal debate as the weather shifts.

17a **ki[u]uetlauc diffrint**: Ms. *kinuetlauc*. This is probably an adj. related to the verb *cywaethlu* 'contend, strive'. This can be taken as valleys are disputed territory, but the rest of the verse consists of nature description. If there is a parallel with 18a *avonit igniw* perhaps the older sense of watercourse would be appropriate for *diffrint*, the waters clashing in spate and wind, but no certain examples of the original sense of *dyffryn* are given in GPC. The suggestion that the second element is *methl* 'snare' has a lot to recommend it: a description of winter valleys being full of snares (heavy snow, downed trees) or treacherous.

c **Llyw in awon**: Both *lliw* 'colour', reflected from clear skies, or *llif* 'flow' or 'spate' from previous rain make sense. In 18 *lliw* is definitely '*llif*', but it is impossible to judge how closely these verses are connected.

18c **neud gueilgi gueled ir eluit**: This line is unclear. The context is a description of flooding. It is difficult to make sense of *gueled* as the vn of *gwelaf* 'I see'. At 8 syllables the line is a bit long. Possibly a scribe accidentally wrote *gue-* twice, creating a plausible word and accidental consonance which masked the error. In which case the line may have read originally *neud gueilgi l[l]ed ir eluit*. The expression *lled yr elfydd/ lled y byd* 'throughout the world' is attested in the works of the Poets of the Princes.

19 This verse is almost certainly intrusive. Like stanzas 8, 30, and 33 it appears elsewhere in the Black Book in a poem collecting stanzas giving the names of the sons of Llywarch Hen (although some like 8 have no personal name in them). See further line c.

a **Nid vid eleic unben**: The rhyme scheme is uncertain here. *Gureic* and *reid* rhyme generically. One would expect *yscoleic* and *eleic* also to rhyme, but *ysgolheic* rhymes with *–ic* in another Black Book poem. Rhyme in the first line of a *englyn penfyr* is not invariable, but line a would be too long if *yscoleic* and *eleic* are 4 syllables and 3 syllables respectively, and the apparent rhyme with *–eid* in lines b and c would be quite a coincidence. Verses about Llywarch's sons seem to have been codified and composed to quite a late date, so this verse may not be as early as the poem in which it was inserted. *Eleic* is probably an error for *elleic*, a rare adj. 'grey'. The only reasonable excuses for a man not being a warrior in this verse are old age or being in holy orders.

c **och Gindilic**: In the genealogical tract called *Bonedd yr Arwyr* the section listing the children of Llywarch Hen includes 'Dilig', probably an error for Cynddylig. This verse has all the hallmarks of Llywarch's castigating of his sons, noting that the subject lacks excuses for not being a warrior, and ending in the ultimate reproach he should have been born a woman. It fits loosely with the theme of reluctance to go to battle, particularly the excuse of advancing age (6b) but is far too extreme to form part of a debate.

20c **Ry dieigc glev o lauer trum**: This is the use of the preverb *ry* for possibility again; cf. 1c. This last gnomic expression of the ability of the bold to escape in dire straits seems to mark the resolution of the internal debate; there may be a subtle closing evocation of the first stanza in the use of *ry* of possibility.

21a **Bronureith breith bron:** This is an odd stanza, in contents and metrically. Not all species of thrush in the British Isles are migratory, but it is not an obvious bird to evoke in a winter description. Lines a and b are an example of *attroi*, repetition in reverse sometimes found in short-line poems, but particularly meaningless here since the descriptive phrase merely echoes the words of the compound which form the bird's name in Welsh.

c **briuhid tal glan gan garn carv culgrum cam**: This intrusive verse may have been inspired by the previous stanza's *briuhid ia* and *carv crum*. It is very close to the striking image found in 'Gwên and Llywarch' 8b *rac carn cann tal glann a vriw*, used to cast doubt on the solidity of intentions there but apparently purely descriptive here. Lines c, d, and e could form an irregular *englyn penfyr*, but if either *glan* or *garn* (generic rhyme) is the *gwant* the pattern is highly irregular and the line rather long. The remaining two lines seem loosely based on stanza 2.

22a **Kalan gaeaw**: This opening is not out of keeping with the winter setting of this poem, but it is also an opening formula found in two purely gnomic poems. Nevertheless, it seems to form the opening of the next part of the poem, or cycle of poems. In saga poems in dialogue form it is usual to find a regular pattern of one speaker to a verse, with an equal number of verses each; cf. poem I, 'Gwên and Llywarch'. If 22 is spoken to Pelis by the narrator of the previous poem, stanzas 22–29 meet this regular pattern. The other stanzas given over to the narrator, however, have a vocative address to Pelis in line c. Line c looks like the resolution of the ongoing debate, addressed directly to Pelis who had proposed the unseasonal expedition. Note how 24 also begins with nature description, and falling and lying snow is alluded to in 25 and 26, providing a link at the start of the dialogue to the previous material.

23a **a[r] aral goruit**: The ms. has *ac* which is probably an error for *ar*, but could be understood as 'with'.

24a There appears to be a short nominal description omitted here after *kinteic guint* which would make a regular *penfyr* stanza.

c **Pelis**: Pelis is otherwise unknown, although there are clues to his identity in the poem. Pelis is the guide on the expedition, a follower of Owain Rheged who was also raised by Owain. He is the defender of the host of Cynwyd (see below 28b), and is familiar with the horse of Pasgen m. Urien. These details seem to place the story in the territory of the men of the Old North of of the British past, although unfortunately the place-names Bryn Tyddwl and (?) Nuchain cannot be identified. Iwerydd in 30a is also uncertain in location and possibly belongs to another interpolated verse.

Llywarch's story is linked to that of his cousin Urien, Owain's father; see I.11a. In a verse interpolated in the *Gododdin*, *CA XLIX*, Cenau fab Llywarch, possibly Llywarch Hen, is credited with rescuing the poet Aneirin from imprisonment, recalling the reason for the expedition in this poem suggested by 29a. It is far from clear, however, whether Pelis's companion was originally a son of Llywarch Hen, and especially whether he is Mechydd, whose *marwnad* follows the dialogue. Mechydd according to 34a was killed in battle with Mwng Mawr Drefydd, an English leader associated with early Anglo-Saxon rulers in a 12th c. genealogical tract, *Bonedd y Saint*. Around 1600 Siôn Dafydd Rhys identified Mwng as a legendary giant whose fortress was in Brycheiniog. This might be dismissed as relocation of legendary northern figures to Wales except that the area is associated with the development of the story of Llywarch Hen and his heroic sons; see I.1c above. The description of Mechydd as a 'youth' in 34b accords with the early deaths of Llywarch's sons and does not match the hints in the dialogue that the narrator is a seasoned, even aging, warrior. The story of rescue from imprisonment, the link of Llywarch's story to that of Urien Rheged, the theme of wisdom versus foolhardiness, and a general tendency perhaps to associate shadowy local heroes with the numerous sons of Llywarch Hen all may have led to a composite text and interpolations such as 19, and perhaps eventual association of the tale with Mechydd. In the collection 'Enweu Meibon Llywarch Hen' elsewhere in the Black Book four stanzas from 'Llym Awel' are included.

Note the typical pattern of the *englynion* dialogues can picked out clearly here. Each speaker has a single verse. As is more typical of some of the antiquarian dialogues the lavish address to Pelis by name clarifies the speakers, and places the spotlight on the character addressed who provides most of the information. The lack of a such a pattern in the first section, even allowing for interpolations, reinforces the interpretation that it is a monologue.

enuir: The adj. < *an-* (neg) + *gwir* meaning 'wicked, false' clearly does not suit the context. There is evidence for a homonym with the prefix *an-*, an intensifier, 'loyal, very true'. See also III.8b.

25a **Kin:** This conjunction is a back formation from *cy(t)* + *ny*; see GMW, p. 235.

hid in Aruul Melin: The name and ownership of this horse is preserved in the Triads of the Island of Britain, in the series usually known as 'Trioedd y Meirch'. TYP 43 names Arfwl Melyn as one of the three pack-horses of the Island of Britain, and says he was the horse of Pasgen m. Urien, a brother of Owain Rheged who is named in 29c as Pelis's lord. The name means 'huge yellow one', his size emphasizing just how deep the snow could be without hindering Pelis. *Hid in* implying 'up to (the height of)' is possible, but may represent *hid tin* 'up to the rump'.

26a **Can medrit ...<y> rodwit a rid — a[r] riv:** The text requires minor emendation here, but there is more than one possibility. *Y* is unlikely to be the preposition 'to' since *medru* usually takes a direct object or the preposition *ar*. If *y* is not intrusive it could be taken as the definite article reading 'y rhodwydd a'r rhyd' and assuming an *r* had been omitted before *riv*; if the *y* is intrusive a second *r* before *rid* is unnecessary. The two types of ford would be difficult to find under snow, but not a slope, so it is unlikely there is a series of three all with the definite article as required by Welsh syntax (*y rodwit a'r rid a'r riv*). If a second *r* was omitted before *riv*, this time giving the preposition *ar*, there is a parenthetical phrase on the hindering weather up on the slope which makes Pelis's abilities finding features in the river valleys all the more impressive.

27a **Ni'm guna pryder:** A restatement of Pelis's lack of worry despite harsh conditions made in 25ab.

heno: The use of *heno* and *heddiw* to add immediacy is a common saga feature, placing us in the heat of the expedition. It is probably intended to rhyme with *bro* in the following line, so earlier *henoeth* can be excluded.

b **bro priw Uchein:** *Uchein* is uncertain. Ifor Williams first noted that a poem from the Book of Taliesin links Owain Rheged to a battle of *nuchien*, with the rhyme scheme indicating the word should be *nuchein*, almost certainly a place-name. *Prif* here could be used as a noun, 'lord', and *uchein* emended to *nuchein*. However, the general statement *im pridein* in line a may indicate Pelis is not speaking of a precise place he would follow Owain, but rather anywhere. The form could also be interpreted as *priu uithein* with t̲ misread as c̲. In that case, comparing *adwyth*, a compound of *gwyth*, which has an attested pl. ending *–ein*, 'the country of the chief hostile ones/ enemies.'

28b kad Kynuid: Cynwyd is attested as both a personal and place name. This could refer to Pelis's fame at a battle at Cynwyd, but it is more likely that Pelis was the hero or warleader of the host of the Cynwydion named in the genealogical tract *Bonedd Gwŷr y Gogledd*, related to the hero Cynwyd Cynwydion named in TYP 6. The evidence that the descendants of Cynwyd were allied to Urien and his sons is explored in EWSP, pp. 99–100, and the alternative theories about a battle at a place called Cynwyd on pp. 238–39.

29b rut y par o penaeth: *Rhudd ei bar* is a descriptive phrase which usually directly follows the noun modified; see GMW, p. 37. With *o bennaeth* here it indicates the type of leader Owain is.

c a'm ry vaeth: Ifor Williams suggests the use of *ry* here is to avoid confusion with the noun, *maeth*. It is largely neutral. For the placing of the preverb *a* (with the infixed object pronoun here) before *ry* see GMW, p. 62. This would be a later usage.

30 Stanza 29 marks the end of the clear dialogue with Pelis, and suggests the reason for the dangerous unseasonal expedition is to deliver Owain from imprisonment. The remaining stanzas are of uncertain relationship to the opening and the dialogue, and all or several may be added to the poem. A clear *marwnad* for Mechydd mab Llywarch is found in 31, 32, 34, 35 and 36, conforming to the usual pattern of the saga *marwnad* in naming the mourned person in every stanza, although this pattern elsewhere can be broken in introductory or concluding verses. The most likely narrator for the *marwnad* would be Llywarch Hen, a new voice, and only relevant to the previous material if Mechydd was Pelis's companion, as seems unlikely. Llywarch might fit the supposed advanced age of the speaker in the opening, but his character is not presented as exercizing caution and deliberation, and Mechydd's death at any rate is hard to link to the expedition to rescue Owain. Stanzas 30 and 35 concern battle at the ford perhaps inspired by 26a. Stanza 35 in particular resembles the opening material, but since it describes battle joined it seems hard to connect to either the debate or dialogue. Stanza 33 also describes a battle with new names introduced.

30a rod[wi]t Iwerit: This unidentified place-name may lie in the Old North and be connected with a story told about Rhun m. Maelgwn; see EWSP, pp. 236–37. The verse seems to concern reluctance to give battle, but on the part of a warband, not the leader. This somewhat related theme, plus the reference to yet another ford could explain its inclusion here if interpolated.

c The appeal here is to the heroic contract of paying for mead which is thematically prominent in the *Gododdin* and elsewhere. The warriors by accepting their leader's mead promise implicitly to fight boldly for him. They would be shamed for breaking this vow if they fled. In the story about Rhun the halt of the warband at the ford is ascribed to a more respectable disagreement about the rights of precedence of various parts of the army.

31b **Mug Maur Treuit**: See above, 24c. This stanza marks the beginning of a *marwnad* to Mechydd m. Llywarch, excluding verses 33 and 35. Mechydd appears in the *Bonedd yr Arwyr* lists as a son of Llywarch Hen, and the same name is found for a grandson of Llywarch in another tract.

32a **Ni'm guna lleuenit**: The similarity to the opening of verse 27 may have encouraged the interpolation of the *marwnad*. The sentiment also recalls that in the three Juvencus *englynion* about the inability of drink to do its usual lightening of spirit in sad circumstances.

33 **Kyuaruuan am cavall**: Words which mean 'to encounter, meet' can also mean 'to fight' in Middle Welsh; cf. *cyfranc* in line c. GPC lists the sense 'battle' for *cyfarfod* as a noun, but not as a verb, although it might suit better than 'meet' here. The final /nt/ of the verbal ending has become assimilated to /nn/ here. Cafall, a borrowing from Latin *caballus* 'horse', is the name of Arthur's dog in the *Historia Brittonum*. Here it is probably the common noun. Either the fighting took place around the steed (of Rhun?), or another special horse.

c **Run**: The ever-increasing cast of characters supports the idea of interpolation here. Rhun is a fairly common name. One candidate would be a brother of Owain Rheged of this name, but he is not well-attested. If this stanza is linked to stanza 30 Rhun m. Maelgwn is far more probable; see above and TYP, p. 503. Those who fought around a horse could be the reluctant warband at Iwerydd of stanza 30, but the despised or disregarded corpse and the identity of '*y drud arall*' ('the other bold one') are both unclear. In the next verse Mechydd is called a '*drudwas*' which could explain the location of this verse if it originally was inserted as a pair with 30.

34b **druduas ni's amgiffredit**: The four stanzas of the *marwnad* to Mechydd seem to break the usual pattern of having the speaker progress from 3rd sg. to direct address of the dead, giving no help with sorting the tense and person of *amgiffredit*. The ending could be the pres./fut. relative one, but seems to make little sense, as does taking this as the 2nd sg. pres./fut. The very rare 1st sg. pres./fut. ending *–ydd* appears to give the best sense here, in the absence of more context — the speaker cannot take in the death of Mechydd. *Druduas* can be in apposition to Mechydd in the first line or the subject of a relative. If vocative with the 2nd sg. there is no vocative particle. As a further complication, Drudwas is attested as a personal name. Greater knowledge of the story than we have is needed here.

c The line is rather long. Either the affixed 2nd sg. pronoun after *pereist* can be omitted, or *im* substituted for *imi*.

35 As noted above, this stanza seems to have more in common with the opening material, with both stanzas 10 and 22 speaking of *cyngor*. The reference to God and men battling at the ford, however, provides reasons why it could have been interpolated here, or misplaced from the earlier stanzas.

c **rothid**: This could be 3rd sg. impersonal indicative ending added to the subjunctive stem of *rhoddi*. But the 3rd sg. imperative gives better sense; see GMW, p. 129.

36c **kyntaw a ffruinclymus march**: Although fighting on horseback is well attested in early Welsh literature, this refers to Mechydd being the first to descend and tie up his horse in order to rush into battle on foot.

GLOSSARY

All systems for compiling a Middle Welsh vocabulary have their weaknesses or difficulties. A separate entry for every variant spelling, plural or verbal form in the text might speed up mechanical translation. However, it would reduce the ability to grasp the larger picture of the language and be frustrating for those with more familiarity with Welsh. I have chosen in the end to order entries according to how their Medieval Welsh forms *would* appear if transcribed in modern Welsh spelling, following order of the modern Welsh alphabet, since alphabetising according to the medieval orthography raises its own difficulties. Both c̲ and k̲ are under c̲, d̲ for /d/ will be before d̲ for /ð/ — dd in Modern Welsh spelling. Any system will inevitably involve checking one or two different possibilities if the word is unfamiliar. Students of Welsh have to learn to allow for initial mutations in using vocabularies and dictionaries. All entries are under the radical form in the glossary. If a word occurs only once just that form is given; otherwise plurals, comparisons of adjectival, etc., are found under a headword entry. The verbal noun as it appears in the texts or a normalized Middle Welsh spelling of the verbal noun provides the headword for all verbal forms. Where forms are considerably different from the headword cross-references are provided.

With medieval orthography it is often impossible to divide a nasal mutation neatly, giving less than clear headword entries. For *fy* and *yn* the various forms are noted according to spelling conventions with the following radical sound. Infixed and contracted forms are found under the headword of the form to which they are affixed. Almost every word in the text has been included, although inevitably more than one interpretation is possible for some examples and a few totally uncertain words are commented on only in the notes. Entries with 'see note' attached indicate that the form is uncertain and provisional for various reasons. However frustrating, the vocabulary is not extensive for this handful of poems and it should be possible to find a word with a bit of persistence, and occasional help from the notes. Also while the notes rarely discuss matter of simple vocabulary the glossary should not be depended upon exclusively for translation.

Proper Names

Aruul Melin: horse of Pasgen son of Urien IV.25a

Brochuael: early king of Powys III.37b

Caranmael, Karanmael: son of Cynddylan III.92c, III.93a, III.94c, III.95c, III.96a, III.97a

Ceinfryd: sister of Heledd and Cynddylan III.109c

Kynan: brother of Cynddylan III.83b

Kyndrwyn, Cyndrwyn: father of Cynddylan III.8c, III.12c, III.13a, III.58c, III.106b, III.107b

Kyndrwynyn, Kynndrwynin: family of Cyndrwyn, descendants of Cyndrwyn III.32b, III.47b, III.94c

Kynuid [Cynwyd]: hero of the old North? IV.28b see note

Cindilic [Cynddylig]: son of Llywarch Hen? IV.19c see note

Kyndylan, Kynndylan: king of Powys, brother of Heledd III.1b, III.3a-11a, III.13a-16a, III.17c, III.18a-33a, III.28c, III.31c, III.34c, III.41c, III.49c, III.58c, III.79c, III.83b, III.84a, III.94b, III.96b, III.97a, III.99c; *Kyndylan Powys* 'Cynddylan of Powys' III.12a; *Kyndylan Wynn uab Kyndrwyn* 'fair Cynddylan/Cynddylan Wyn son of Cyndrwyn' III.13a; *Kyndylan Wynn* 'fair Cynddylan/Cynddylan Wyn' III.34c, III.47c

Kynon: brother of Cynddylan III.32c

Kynnwreith: brother of Cynddylan III.83b

Eluan: brother of Cynddylan III.28c, III.58b, III.99c; *Eluan Powys* 'Elfan of Powys' note III.31c, III.49c

Ffreuer, Freuer: sister of Cynddylan III.57a-62a, III.65a, III.81b, III.108c; *Ffreuer Wenn* 'fair Ffreuer/ Ffreuer Wen' III.63a, III.64a

Gorwynnyon: see the note to III.80b

Gwen [Gwên]: son of Llywarch Hen I.3c, I.15a-20a, I.21c-27c, II.20b

Gwenddwyn: daughter of Cyndrwyn III.107c

Gwiawn: brother of Cynddylan III.32c

Gwladus: daughter of Cyndrwyn III.107c

Gwledyr: daughter of Cyndrwyn III.109c

Gwyn: brother of Cynddylan III.32c

Heled, Heledd: sister of Cynddylan III.78a, III.79a, III.107c

Llawr: son of Llywarch Hen? II.20b see note

Llywarch Hen: 'Llywarch the Old/ Llywarch Hen' I.24c; *Llywarch* I.28a, II.8c, II.10c, II.21a, IV.36a

GLOSSARY

Mechit: IV.31c see note, IV.32c, IV.34a, *Mechit mab Llywarch* IV.36a
Medlan: sister of Heledd and Cynddylan III.108c
Medwyl: sister of Heledd and Cynddylan III.108c
Meissir, Meysir: sister of Heledd and Cynddylan III.37b, III.109c
Moryal: Powys figure III.77b
Mug Maur Treuit: IV.31b see note; *Mugc* IV.34a
Owein Reged: son of Urien Rheged IV.29c; *Owein* IV.27c
Pelis: warrior from the Old North IV.24c, IV.26c, IV.28c
Run: son of Urien Rheged or Rhun m. Maelgwn IV.33c see note
Vryen: king of Rheged I.11a, I.23b

Place-Names

Argoet: II.1c see note
Argoetwis: n.pl. 'men of Argoed' III.45c
Brynn: place in Powys III.69c
Brin Tytul: unidentified place-name IV.25c
Cymry: 'Wales' II.2c
Dinlleu Ureconn: 'The Wrekin' III.81a see note
Dwyryw: the two branches of the river Rhiw see note III.71b
Dyffrynt Meissir: place in Powys III.37b
Eglwysseu Bassa: burial place in Powys of Cynddylan III.45a–51a
Eli: place in Powys III.34a-39a
Ercal: Ercall in Shropshire III.77a
Gorsed Orwynnyon: 'The Mound of Gorwynnion' III.80b see note
Gyrthmwl: place in Powys III.76a
Hafren: 'The Severn' III.71a
Iwerit: unidentified place IV.30a see note
Llawen: river name I.15a, I.16a, I.17a
Lloegyr: 'England', I.12a, 'men/warriors of England' I.24c
Lloegyrwys: n.pl. 'men/warriors of England' III.15b, III.16b, III.31b, III.49b
Penngwern: court of Cynddylan III.1c, III.40a-44a
Powys: kingdom/region in Wales II.2c, III.12a; as an epithet III.31c, III.49c
Pridein: 'Britain' IV.27a

78 GLOSSARY

Reged: kingdom in North Britain used as an epithet IV.27c

Traual: place in Powys? III.56a see note

Trebwll: place in Powys III.14c

Trenn, Tren: place in Cynddylan's kingdom from the river name, now the Tern in Shropshire III.3c-6c, III.16b, III.43c, III.44c, III.55a, III.56a, III.70c, III.83c, III.104c-106c

Trodwyd: place in Powys? III.55a see note

Uchein, Nuchein: unknown place IV.27b see note

Y Drefwenn: place in Powys III.52a-56a see note

a,b

a: preverbal particle I.9b, I.19a, III.7c, III.36a, IV.16c, IV.26b, IV.34a; with 1st sg. infixed obj. pron. *a'm* II.1c, II.2b, II.9b, II.10b, III.27a, III.33a, III.50c, III.62c, IV.29c; with 2nd sg. infixed obj. pron *a'th* I.5a, I.5b, III.63a; with 3rd sg. infixed obj. pron. *a'e* III.46b, III.86b, with 3rd pl. obj. pron *a'i* III.108b, III.109b; with 1st sg. dat. infixed pron. *a'm* III.19c, III.20c, III.79a, IV.32b; with 1st sg. dat. infixed pron. and *bot* for possession *a'm* I.25a-27a, III.29c, III.85a, III.86a, III.104a, III.105a, III.106b, III.108a, III.109a; with 2nd sg. dat. infixed pron and *bot* for possession **a**'*th* III.64a

a: rel. particle, pron. I.8a, I.11a, I.13b, II.4c, II.10b, II.11c, II.12c, II.15a, III.1d, III.3b, III.3c, III.33b, III.40c, III.42c, III.62a, III.85b, III.86a, III.87c, III.95b, III.98c, IV.29a, IV.36c; with 1st sg. infixed obj. pron. *a'm* II.18c, III.59a, III.61a; with 2nd sg. infixed obj. pron. *a'th* I.18c; with 3rd sg. m. obj. pron. *a'e* III.39c; with 3rd sg. f. obj. pron. *a'e* III.29c; with 3rd pl. obj. pron. *a'e* III.87b; with 1st sg. dat. pron. *a'm* III.60a, III.61b, with 2nd sg. dat. *a'th* I.11a, with 3rd sg. dat. pron. *a'e* III.21c; with 1st sg. dat. pron and *bot* for possession *a'm* III.29b

a: vocative particle I.3c, IV.30b

a: see *o* prep. I.29a, II.21a

a: particle in adjectival construction II.21a see note

a, ac: conj. 'and' I.10b, I.23b, II.15b, II.16c, III.1a, III.2a, III.31c, III.32c, III.49c, III.50c, III.51b, III.55a, III.56a, III.58c, III.61c, III.65a, III.72a, III.72b, III.77c, III.78c, III.95a, III.97b, III.101a, III.101b, III.104b, III.105b, III.107c-109c, IV.26a see note, IV.28a; with contracted definite article *a'r* I.16b, I.17b, II.11c, II.12c, IV.33c; with 1st sg. possessive pron. *a'm* III.62c; with 2nd sg. possessive pron. *a'th* I.14b; with 3rd sg. m. possessive pron. *a'e* I.11b, III.79c

a, ac: prep. 'with' II.11b, II.12a, IV.23b

Glossary

abar: n.m. 'carcass, corpse' II.20c
ac a: III.2c see note
achadw: 'guard, keep', 3rd sg. pres./fut. *echeidw* III.38a
achen: n.f. 'lineage' I.3b
aches: n.m. 'tide, flow' I.22a
achlan: adv. 'wholly, entirely' III.108b
adar: pl. 'birds' IV.12a
adaf: n.f. (1) 'hand', *ech adaf* I.7b see note; (2) 'talon' III.42b
a dan: prep. 'under' III.53c
adaw: 'leave', 1st sg. pret. *edeweis* III.92a see note
adei: III.11a see note
adfer: 'return, restore', 3rd sg. pres./fut. III.10c *atuer* see note
atuot [adfod]: 'be, happen to be', 3rd sg. pres. subjunctive *ytuo, atuo* III.65b, III.66b
atleis [adleis]: n.m. 'cry' III.40b
atnabot [adnabod]: 'recognize, know', 1st sg. pres./fut. *atwen* I.3a, III.93b
adrawd [adrawdd]: n.m. 'story, report' I.15c
atwen: see *atnabot*
athuc [addug]: n. 'attack' I.15b see note
adwyn, addfwyn: adj. 'fair' III.106a, III.107a
ae...ae: interrogative 'whether it is ... or ... or' III.91a, III.91b
aeleu: n.f. 'pain, suffering' III.101a
aer: n.f. 'battle, slaughter' III.91, III.92a
awon [afon]: n.f. 'river' IV.17c, pl. *avonit* IV.18a
awirtul [afrddwl]: adj. 'fearful' IV.25b
agdo [angdo]: n. (1) 'thin covering, poor protection' < *ang* adj. 'narrow' + *to* n.m. 'covering' I.7c; (2) 'covering' IV.13a
aghen [anghen]: n.m. (1) 'need' I.11c; (2) 'battle' I.12a
agheu, angheu [angheu]: n.m. 'death' II.19c, III.23c, III.58b, III.59a–62a, III.101a,
anghwyf: see *engi*
anghyuyeith: n.m./ collective 'foreigner, enemy' III.4a see note
angwyr: n.pl. 'warriors' I.12a
alarch: n.m.f. 'swan' IV.36b
allan: adv. 'out, outside' IV.2c, IV.21e; *sefwch allann* III.1a see note

am: prep. (1) 'around' I.10a, I.11b, III.13b, III.14c, IV.11a, IV.33a; 'around' or 'for' ? III.4b see note; (2) 'for' III.15c, III.40c–42c, III.81c; (3) 'because of' III.59b, conjugated 2nd sg. *amdanat* III.20c; (4) *y am* compound prep. 'around' III.71b

amgeled: n.m. 'care, anxiety, concern' III.15c

amgiffred [amgyffred]: 'know, comprehend, understand', 1st sg. pres./fut. ? *amgyffredit* IV.34b see note

amgyhudaw [amgyhuddaw]: 'declare, state, say', 3rd sg. pres./fut. *amgyhud* I.2c

amser: n.m.f. 'time' used as adverb 'at the time, when' III.98a, III.107a

amwyn: 'defend, fight for', vn III.4c, III.83c; 3rd sg. imperf. *amucsei* III.5c, III.6c

amwyth: III.24c see note

an: 1st pl. possessive pron. III.65c

anaw [anaf]: n.m. 'wound, defect, disability' IV.8c

anffawt: n.f. 'misfortune' III.57c, III.86b

anhaut [anhawdd]: adj. 'difficult' IV.1a

annelwic: adj. 'shapeless' II.17a

annwadal: adj. 'fickle, unstable' II.18a

annwar: adj. 'savage, rough, uncouth' II.18b, II.20c

annuyd [annwyd]: n.m. 'nature' IV.9c

ar: demonstrative pron. introducing rel. clause 'those who' III.87c

ar: prep. (1) 'on' I.1a, I.1c, I.7c, I.15c, I.16b, I.17b, I.23c, I.24b, III.24b, III.33c, III.43b, III.44b, III.52c, III.56b, III.77a, III.84a, III.93c, IV.1c, IV.6b, IV.7c, IV.10b, IV.15c, IV.23a, *a[r]* IV.26b see note; conjugated 1st sg. *arnaf* III.36c; 2nd sg. *arnat* III.93a, *arnad* IV.28a, IV.32c; 3rd sg. m. *arnaw* III.2a; (2) with a compound number I.25a, I.26a, I.27a, I.28a, I.29a; (3) 'at' I.5c, II.5b; (4) with *gwall* 'disregarded, despised' IV.33b

araf: adj. 'quiet' III.30a

aral: adj. 'vigorous, lively' IV.23a

arall: adj. 'other' IV.33c

artu [arddu]: n. 'gloom' IV.25b

aren: n.m. 'hoar-frost' IV.6a

aruaeth [arfaeth]: n.m.f. 'intention, purpose, plan' I.7b

ar hyt: prep. 'along' I.7a

arllaw: vn 'sharing, giving' III.96b

armau: 'intend', 1st sg. pres./fut. *armaaf* I.4b, I.10b

GLOSSARY

armeithyd: III.14b see note

aruchel: adj. 'very high' III.40b–42b

ar vnweith: adv. 'at once, at the same time' III.83a

ar warthaw: compound prep. 'on, on top of' IV.7a

ariweu [ar(y)feu]: n. pl. of *arf* 'arms, weapons, armour' IV.28a

arwest: n.f. 'band, ornament' or 'cord' I.11b see note

aruiar [arwyar]: adj. 'bloody, bloodstained' IV.33b

as: syllabic 3rd sg. obj. pron. I.1b see note

asswy: n.f. 'leftside, left' I.1a

awel: n.f. 'wind' I.2b, III.87a, IV.1a, IV.3c, IV.21d

awen: n.f. 'inspiration, mind, heart' I.3a

awr: n.f. 'time'; *pob awr* adv. 'continuously, all the time' III.33a

auir [awyr]: n.f.m. 'air, sky' IV.11b

baglan: n.f. 'little or dear crutch, walking stick', diminutive of *bagl* 'crutch, staff, walking stick' II.4a–10a

ban, bann: adj. 'loud, noisy' III.34a, III.76b

ban: see *pan*

bannev: n.pl. 'summits, peaks, heights' IV.2b

baraf: n.f. 'beard' III.13b

barywhaud: adj. 'bearded' IV.4b

betwn: contraction of *pei yt vwn* < *pei* 'if' + *bewn* 1st sg. imperf. subjunctive of *bot*. Or an orthographic variant for *bydwn* 1st sg. consuetudinal past 'were I' I.20c see note

bed [bedd]: n.m. 'grave' I.24c, III.22b

beidyaw [beiddiaw]: 'defy', 1st sg. pres./fut. *beidyaf* III.36b

bereu: n.pl. 'spears' III.101b

biv [biw]: n.f. and collective 'cow, cattle' IV.9b

blaen: n.m. 'tip, top' IV.7b, IV.11c, IV.22a

bleid [bleidd]: n.m. 'wolf' III.10b

bot: 'be', vn III.71c; 1st sg. pres. *wyf* I.2c, II.3c, II.6c, II.10c, II.17a, II.17c, II.18a, II.18b, II.20c, II.51b; 2nd sg. pres. *wyt, vid* III.14a, IV.19a, IV.26c; 3rd sg. pres. *mae* II.11a, II.12a, III.22b; *oes* III.72c, III.106c; *yw* III.36b, III.57a, III.58a; *eu* I.28c; pres. impersonal *ys* I.18b, III.2b, III.18a–21a, III.23a, III.25a, III.26a, III.28a–32a, III.48b, III.66c; 3rd sg. pres. relative *yssy* II.15a; 3rd pl. pres. *ynt* III.46a, III.46c, III.47a, III.48a, III.48c,

III.50a, III.51a, III.51c; 3rd pl. pres. *ydynt* III.87c; pres. impersonal *yssit, yssyd* I.8a, III.91c; 3rd sg. consuetudinal pres./fut. *byd* II.5b; 1st sg. fut. *bydaf* III.101c; 2nd sg. fut *bydyd* III.14b; 3rd sg. fut. *bit* IV.16c, IV.17c; 2nd sg. imperf. *oedut* I.20b; 3rd sg. imperf. *oed, oet* I.23a, I.23b, I.25c, I.26c, II.3b, III.55b, III.56b, III. 95a, III.95b, III.100c, IV.31c; 3rd pl. imperf. *oedyn* I.27c; 3rd sg. consuetudinal past *bydei* I.13c, III.76a, III.76b; *bwyat* I.26a, III.85a, III.86a, III.99a; *buei* III.29b; 3rd pl. consuetudinal past *bwyn* (for *bwyyn*) I.27a; 1st sg. pret. *bum* I.13a, II.1a, II.2a, II.3a, III.98a; 2nd sg. pret. *buost* IV.19c; 3rd sg. pret. *bu, by* I.14c, I.16c, I.17c, I.19c, I.25a, III.6c, III.22c, III.64a, III.69a, III.70a, III.87c, III.104a, III.108a, III.109a; 3rd pl. pret. *buant* III.105a, III.106b, III.107a; 1st sg. pres./fut. subjunctive *bwyf* I.8b, compounded with *cy(t) cybwyf* I.1a see note; 3rd sg. pres./fut. subjunctive *bo* II.10b, III.13c, IV.13b; 3rd sg. imperf. subjunctive *bei* III.76a; 2nd sg. imperative *byd* II.10b; 3rd sg. imperative *bit* I.2a

bodawc: adj. 'continual' II.8c; *[b]odawc* 'steadfast, staunch' III.28b see note

bore: n.m. 'morning' IV.31a; used adverbally 'in the morning' III.59c

bras: adj. 'abundant, luxurious' III.98a

bre: n.f. 'hill, uplands' II.13b, IV.2b

breit [breidd]: adv. 'scarcely' IV.2c, IV.21e

breint: n.m.f. 'privilege, status, honour' III.49a

breith: adj. 'speckled' IV.21a, IV.21b

briger: n.m.f. 'long hair (of a warrior)' III.100a

brith: adj. 'multi-coloured, dappled' IV.35b

briw: adj. 'broken, shattered' I.10c

briwaw: 'break, injure', vn I.8b see note; 3rd sg. pres./fut. *briw* I.9b; 3rd sg. pres. absolute *briuhid* IV.20b, IV.21c

bro: n.f. 'region, land' IV.27b

broder, brodyr: pl. of *brawd* n.m. 'brother' III.62c, III.63a, III.64a, III.71a, III.78c, III.83a, III.85a, III.86a, III.99a, III.100c, III.104a, III.105a, III.106a,

brodyrde: III.59b, III.81c see notes

brotre: III.1d see note

bronn, bron: n.f. 'breast, slope' III.52a, IV.1a, IV.21.a, IV.21b, IV.35b

bronureith: n.m.f. 'thrush' IV. 21a, IV.21b

brooet: pl. of *bro* n.f. 'region, land' IV.20b

brwyn: adj. 'sorrowful, sad' I.2a

brwyt: adj. 'bloodstained' I.10c

bryt: n.m. 'mind, thought, spirit' I.2a, I.18a

brin [bryn]: n.m. 'hill' IV.1a, IV.12c

brynar: n.m. 'fallow land' III.56c

brythuch: n.m. 'storm, tumult' IV.3a

buch: n.f. 'cow' III.66b

buteir: III.8b see note

bwyt: n.m. 'food' III.98a

bychot: n.m. 'a little' I.29c

byt: n.m. 'world'; *gwynn y byt* III.57a, III.58a see *gwynn*

bydeir: III.54b see note

bygylaeth: n.m. 'fear, cowardice' III.63c

birr, bir [byr]: adj. 'short' IV.4b, IV.11c, IV.22c

byrr: interrogative 'why' III.23c

byth: adv. 'ever' III.84b

byw, buw: adj. 'living, alive' III.27c; *yn vyw* 'alive' I.14b, III.71c

bywyt: n. 'means' ? III.12b see note

c

kat, cat, cad, kad: n.f. (1) 'battle' I.7c, III.7c, III.9c, III.11c, III.45c, III.54b, III.55b, III.65b, III.93b; IV.8b; (2) 'host, army, troop' I.26b, III.5b, IV.28b see note

catpeis: n.f. 'battle cloak' III.97a

kadir: adj. 'fine, comely' IV.7c

kadw: 'keep, care for, hold', 3rd sg. imperf. *katwei* III.29c

kadwynawc: adj. 'wearing an ornamental chain' III.5b, III.6b

kaeawc: adj. 'wearing a brooch/ diadem' III.28c

caer: n.f. 'fortress' I.10a

caeth: adj. 'confined, stringent' IV.29a

kaeu: 'close, block, defend', 2nd sg. imperative *keu* III.15a, III.16a

cavall: n.m. 'horse, steed' IV.33a see note

caffael: 'get, obtain' vn IV.1a; 3rd sg. imperf. *caffei* III.97c

canghen: n.f. 'branch' II.8a, II.9a

kalaf, calaw: collective n. 'reeds, stalks' II.4b, IV.3b, IV.14b

kalan gaeaw: n.m. 'the first of November, the first day of winter' IV.22a

calaned, kalaned: see *celain*

kalet, caled: adj. 'hard, solid' I.9a, II.9a, III.69a, III.70a, IV.14b

callon [cal-lon]: n.f. (1) 'heart, spirit' III.3a, III.4a, III.7a–9a, III.11b, III.17a, III.34c, III.45c; (2) 'emotions, feeling' III.48c

callet [calledd]: n.pl. 'trees, grove' IV.17c

cam: adj. 'crooked, bent' IV.21c

can, kan: conj. 'because, since' I.16c, I.17c, I.19c, IV.26a, IV.30a,

can: cardinal number 'one hundred' III.17c

cann, can: adj. 'white' used as a substantive 'white horse' I.9b, IV.27c

cannwyll: n.f. 'candle' III.19c

canis: conj. 'since, because' IV.34a

kanlin: vn 'following' IV.27c

car: n.m. 'relation, friend' I.18c

carchar: n.m. 'prison' IV.29a

karcharaur: n.m. 'prisoner' IV.9b

carn: n.m. 'hoof' I.9b, IV.21

carrec: n.f.m. 'rock, stone' III.24b

caru, karu: 'love', 1st sg. pres./fut. *caraf* II.4c, III.42c; 3rd sg. pres./fut. *kar* II.18c, II.19a; 3rd pl. imperf. *cerynt* II.11c, II.12c; impersonal imperf. *cerid* III.107b; 1st sg. pret. *cereis* II.15a, III.40c; 3rd sg. pret. *karawd* II.18c

carv, caru [carw]: n.m. 'stag, deer' IV.20a, IV.21c, IV.24b

cas: adj. 'hateful, disagreeable' II.15a

casnar: n.m. ? 'enemy, warrior' or ? 'grief, pain' I.18c see note

kassulwin: adj. 'having a white cloak' IV.12c

caun: n.pl. 'stalks, reeds' IV.3b, IV.4b, IV.24b, sg. *conin* IV.1c

ketwyr, cetwyr, keduir: n.pl. 'warriors' III.28b, III.50b, III.91b, IV.8b

kedyrn: pl. of adj. *cadarn* 'mighty, strong' used as substantive n. III.92b

kedic: adj. 'angry, wrathful' IV.3c

kewin [cefyn]: n.m. 'ridge' IV.12c

keuyngrwm: adj. 'bent-back' II.3c

kein-vaglawc, kein-uaglawc: n.m. 'bent-backed' II.1a–3a

keinmic: adj. 'splendid, honourable, praiseworthy' II.17b

ceinmygu: 'admire', impersonal pres. indicative? *keinmygyr* II.1b see note

ceissyaw: 'seek', 3rd sg. pret. *ceissyws* III.95c

Glossary

keithiv: n.m. 'captivity' IV.14a

kelein: n.f. 'corpse, body' IV.33b, pl. *calaned, kalaned* III.7c, III.9c; *llad celain* see *llad*

kelyn: collective n. 'holly' III.69b

kelyngar: adj. 'fond of holly, eager for holly' III.70b

kell: n.f. 'store-house' III.12b

keneu: n.m. 'whelp, son, descendant' III.8c, III.12c

kenueint [cenfeint]: n.f. 'family' I.28a, III.57b

kenniret: see *kynniret*

kerdeu: n.pl. 'songs' III.25b

cev [ceu]: adj. 'hollow' IV.15b

keugant: adj. 'undoubted, certain' III.105c

kic: n.m. 'flesh' III.40c–42c

kildynnawc: adj. 'stubborn, obstinate' III.5b see note

kinyawa: vn 'dining, eating' III.39b

claf: n.m. 'sick person' III.98c see note

clawd: n.m. 'bank, earthwork' I.10a, I.15c

cledyr: n.f. 'pillar, post' III.45c

cleuyt [clefyd]: n.m. 'illness, disease' III.99b

clot: n.m.f. 'fame, renown, praise' I.28c, III.94b, III.96b

cloyn [clöyn]: n.m. 'protuberance, rod' II.11c, II.12c

cluir [clwyr]: IV.11a see note

clid [clyd] (1) n.m. 'shelter, warmth' IV.1a; (2) adj. 'sheltered' IV.20a

clidur: n.m. 'shelter, warmth, protection' IV.15a

clywet: 'hear', 1st sg. pres./fut. *clywaf* III.36a; 3rd pl. imperf. *clywynt* III.64b

knawt: n.m. 'flesh' I.29a

cnes: n.m. 'surface' IV.5a

coch: adj. 'red' IV.12c, III.61c

cochwed: adj. 'red' compound of *coch* adj. 'red' + *gwedd* n.f.m. 'aspect' III.72a

codi [coddi]: 'trouble, hurt, harm', imperf. impersonal *codet* III.37c

coet, coed: collective n. (1) 'wood, forest' III.16c, III.35c, III.36c, III.39a, III.52a, IV.24a; (2) 'trees' IV.3c see note

coes: n.f.m. 'leg' III.72c

couyon: n.pl. 'memories, recollections' III.80c

cogeu: n.pl. 'cuckoos' II.6b

coll: collective n. 'hazel trees' III.85b

colli: 'lose', vn III.30b, III.57b; 1st sg. pres./fut. *collaf* I.6a; 1st sg. pret. *collais* III.108b, III.109b; 3rd sg. pret. *colles* I.22c; 3rd pl. pret. *collassant* III.49a; pl. impersonal pret. *colledeint* I.29c; 2nd sg. imperative *coll* I.5c

conin: see *caun*

corn: n.m. 'horn' I.11a; pl. *cirn* IV.11a

cornwyt: n.m. 'boil, abcess, plague' III.98c see note; pl. *cornnwydeu* III.99b

creilum: compound adj. 'bare, exposed' IV.24a

creu: n.m. 'blood' III.34c

creulyt: adj. 'bloodstained, gory' III.36b

crin: adj. 'withered, brittle' IV.3b, IV.14b, IV.24b

croenen: n.f. 'skin' III.69a, III.70a

crum [crwm]: adj. 'bowed, bent' IV.20a

crych: adj. 'curly' II.7b

cu: adj. as substantive n. 'dear thing'? III.3c see note

cul: adj. 'narrow, thin' IV.4b, IV.9b, IV.17b

culgrum: compound adj. 'thin and bowed' IV.21c

culhwch: n. 'boar' or adj. 'boar-like'? III.10a see note

cunlleit: collective n. 'fresh grass, herbage'? IV.15b see note

cwl: n.m. 'fault, wrong, sin' I.28c

cum: n.m. 'valley, glen' IV.20a

cwrwf: n.m. 'beer, ale' III.3c, III.11c

kwyn: n.m. 'supper, evening meal' I.2a

cwyn: n.m.f. 'lament, complaint' II.6b

cwynaw: (1) 'lament', 1st sg. pres./fut. *cwynif* I.5b, *cwynaf* III.62c; impersonal pres./fut. *cwynitor* III.12c; (2) 'complain of, bemoan' 3rd sg. imperf. *cwynei* III.98c; (3) 'suffer from'? 3rd sg. imperf. *cwynei* III.99b

cybwyf: see *bod*

kyt: conj. 'although' III.65b, III.66a, III.96c

cyua [cyfa]: adj. 'whole' III.76b

kyuadas: adj. 'suitable, appropriate, fitting' II.15c

cyuamrud: n.m. 'confusion, slaughter, bloodshed' or adj. 'bloody' III.54b

kyuamwc: vn 'contending, fighting' III.91b

GLOSSARY

cyfarch: 'greet, address', 3rd sg. pres./fut. *kyueirch* III.79a

cyfaruot: 'meet, come together', 3rd pl. imperf.? *cyueruydynt* II.16b see note, 3rd pl. or 1st pl. pret. *kyuaruuan* IV.33a see note

kyvarwit: n.m. 'guide' or adj. 'well-informed, expert' IV.26c

kyueirch: see *cyfarch*

cyflwyn: n.m. 'gift' III.4b

kyuor: adj. 'complete, full' III.39b

kywranc: n.m.f. 'clash, encounter' IV.33c

kyuyrdy: n.m. 'alehouse, drinking hall' II.2b

cywryssed: n.m.f. 'conflict, battle, strife' III.100b

cyfwyf: *kyt* + *bod*, 1st sg. pres. subjunctive I.1a

cyffes-eiryawc: 'ready with words, eloquent' II.1a

kyghor, kighor [cynghor]: n.m. 'counsel, advice, deliberation' IV.10c, IV.22c, IV.35c

kyngran: n.m. 'warrior' III.17c

cyngrwn: adj. 'compact, hunched' I.24b

kylchet: n.m. 'coverlet, bedclothes' III.69a, III.70a

kymelri: n.m.f. 'commotion, tumult' III.7b

kymwed [cymŵedd]: vn 'joke, jest, mock' II.11a, II.12a

kymwed: n.m. 'joke, jest' III.94a, III.96a

kymwy: n.m. 'stress, affliction, trouble' III.93a

kymwyat: n.m. 'tormentor, warrior' III.14a

kynn, kin: conj. 'before' I.6c, I.10c, II.1a–3a, III.69a, III.70a; IV.28a

kin: IV.25a see *cyt*

kynndynnyawc, kyndynyawc: adj. 'unyielding' III.6b, III.8c

cynndeiryawc: adj. 'raging, furious' III.8b

cynhayaf: n.m. 'harvest-time, autumn' II.4a

kynhelych: see *cynnal*

cynnifiat, kyniuiat: n.m. 'warrior' III.10a, III.93c

kynniret: (1) 'go to and fro, get about, visit', vn II.9c; (2) 'drive to and fro', 3rd sg. pres./fut. *kenniret* II.14a; (3) 'visit, frequent' 3rd sg. pres./fut. *kenniret* II.19a

cynnal: 'support, hold up, sustain', 2nd sg. subjunctive *kynhelych* II.8b, II.10b

cynnu: 'fall', vn or 3rd sg. pres./fut. III.26c see note

kynnyt: conj. *kyt* + negative preverbal particle I.4c see note

kynrein: pl. of *cynran* n.m. 'warrior' I.21b, I.22b

kyntaw: adj. as substantive n. 'the first one' IV.36c

kynteuin: n.m. 'early summer' II.7a

kinteic: adj. 'strong, keen' IV.24a

kynwaew: n.m.f. 'spear, vanguard spear' < *cyn-* prefix 'first' + *gwaew* II.3b

kynwan: n.m. 'one who draws first blood' from *cyn-* prefix 'first' + *gwân* n.m.f. 'thrust, blow, attack' II.3b

kynnwys: 'include, welcome', 3rd sg. pres./fut. *kynnwyss* II.9b; impersonal imperf. *kynnwyssit* II.2b

kyrchu: (1) 'make for', vn IV. 27b; 3rd sg. pres. absolute (2) 'make for, haunt' *kirchid* IV.20a; pret. impersonal *kirchuid* IV.31b

cirn: see *corn*

kisscaud, kiscaud: n.m. 'shadow, shelter, refuge' IV.4a, IV.23a

kysylltu: vn 'connecting, joining' III.17b

cyweithyd: n.f. 'company, host' III.21b

kiuuetlauc: adj. 'disputed, contending'? IV.17a see note

kywir: adj. 'true, faithful' II.9c

kywlat: n.f.m. 'borderland' or 'fellow-countryman' III.5a

cywrenin: adj. 'skilful, powerful' III.64b

ch, d

chwannawc: adj. 'desirous, greedy' III.69b, III.70b

chuetleu: pl. of *chwedl* n.m.f. 'news, stories' IV.32b

chwerw: adj. 'bitter, painful, spiteful, hurtful' I.2b

chwiorydd: pl. of n.f. *chwaer* 'sister' III.108a, III.109a

chwythu: 'blow', 2nd sg. imperative *chwyth* I.11c

da: adj. 'good' I.29c, comparative *gwell* II.10b, III.13c; superlative *goreu* I.25c, I.26c, III.92c; substantive n. 'good' III.21c

dagreu, deigyr: n. pl. 'tears' III.25c, III.26c, III.61c

damorth: uncertain III.59b see note, III.81c

dan: in compound prep. *a dan* 'under' III.53c

danned: pl. of *dant* n.m. 'tooth' II.12b

darfot: (1) 'happen, occur', 3rd sg. imperative *derffit* III.2c; (2) 'come to pass, be accomplished', 3rd sg. imperative *deruhid* IV.22c; (3) 'perish, die', 3rd pl. perf. *derynt* III.54c

darymret: vn 'wander to and fro, visit, walk about' II.19b

daw: see *dyfot*

de: 3rd sg. pres./fut. of defective verb 'burn, pain, hurt' III.59a

dechreu: n.m. 'beginning' III.60b

dedwyd: adj. 'happy, fortunate, wise' I.20c see note

deigyr: see *dagreu*

deilen: n.f. 'leaf' II.14a

deint: pl. of *dant* n.m. 'tooth' II.11b

deu: cardinal number 'two' III.99c

deudrwch: n.m. 'two layers' III.9c

deurudd: n.pl. (dual) 'cheeks' III.25c

deweint: n.m. 'end of night, dead of night' III.60b

dewr, deur: adj. 'bold, brave, strong' II.13b, IV.23b

di: affixed auxiliary pron. 2nd sg. I.11a, III.15a, III.16a; see also *ti, (t)e*

diallad: see *dyall*

dianc: 'escape', 2nd sg. pres./fut. *diegyd* I.5a; 3rd sg. pres./fut. *dieinc, dieigc* III.2b, IV.20c; 2nd sg. imperf. subjunctive *dianghut* I.20c

diannerch: adj. 'without greetings' II.5c

diarchar: adj. 'mighty, valiant' IV.23b

didan: adj. 'pleasant, delightful' III.108a

dien: n. 'grass' IV.6c

diua [difa]: adj. 'destroyed, devastated' III.50a, III.76c

diua, dyua: vn 'destroying, killing' III.49b, III.31b

difot: 'be of worth, avail', 3rd sg. pres./fut. *diw* I.9c, III.15c

diffaeth: adj. 'perverse, stubborn, wicked' III.63b

difawt: adj. 'misfortunate' III.43c

diffeith: adj. 'uninhabited, laid to waste' III.4c see note, III.83c

diffret: n.m. 'defense, protection' II.9b

diffreidad: n.m. 'defender, protector' IV.28b

digarat: adj. (1) 'rejected, unliked' II.6c; (2) 'forsaken, forlorn' III.23a

digaru: 'reject, turn away from, dislike', 1st sg. pret. *digereis* II.4c

digwyd: 'falls, occurs', 3rd sg. pres./fut. *diguit* IV.26b

digyuyng: adj. 'wide, not narrow' III.92b

dihat: adj. 'without progeny' III.95a see note

dihawarch [dihafarch]: adj. 'brave, bold' IV.36a

diheid: adj. 'wretched' III.95a

diheint: adj. 'painful, afflicting' III.57a

diheu: adv. 'doubtless, certainly' I.14a

diholedic: adj. 'exiled' III.95b

dilin: vn 'following, pursuing' III.10b

dillat: collective n. 'garments, clothing' III.72a

dinas: n.f. 'stronghold, fortress' III.92c

diruawr: adj. 'very great' III.100b

dirper: 'deserve, merit, earn', 3rd sg. pres./fut. *dirper* III.100a

disgynnu: 'descend, attack', 3rd sg. imperf. *disgynnei* III.7b, III.9b

disgynnyat: n.m. 'attacker' III.10b

disgyr: n.f. 'cry, wail' III.76b

disgywen: adj. 'splendid, manifest' I.23a

diw: see *difot*

diuedit, diwedit [diwedydd]: n.m. 'end of day, nightfall' IV.4c, IV.11c

diwed: adj. 'last' III.45b

diwedwr: n.m. 'rear guard warrior' III.94b

diweir: adj. 'reliable, honest, true' I.14a

diwlyd, divlit [diwlydd]: adj. 'rough, hard, unkind' II.13b, IV.14c

diulit: IV.12b see note

draw: demonstrative adv. 'yonder, over there' I.13a

dros: prep. 'over' III.61c

drut, drud: adj. 'foolish' II.18a; as substantive n. 'brave one, hero, reckless one' IV.33c

drudwas: n.m. 'brave lad, youth' IV.34a

drwc: adj. 'bad, grievous' III.91c

drwy, trwy: prep. 'through' I.29b, III.3b, III.16b

driccin [drycin]: n.f.m. 'stormy weather, bad weather' IV.18a

dricweuet [drygfeuedd]: n.m. 'ill possession, bad possession' IV.15c

du: adj. 'black' III.17b

duc: see *dwyn*

duhunaw: 'awaken', 1st sg. pres./fut. ***duhunaf*** I.12c, III.60c, III.61c

Duw, Duv: n.m. 'God' II.9b, III.2c, III.19c, III.30c, III.71c, III.78b, III.79a, III.86a, IV.29a; ***Duw gennyt*** I.4c 'God be with you, farewell'

duvin [dwfyn]: adj. 'deep, mysterious' IV.35c

dwylan: pl. (dual) of *glan* 'banks' III.71b

dwyn: (1) 'bear, carry off', vn III.66b; (2) 'take' ***duc*** 3rd sg. pret. III.86a

dy: 2nd sg. possessive pron. 'your' I.2a, I.6a, I.14a, I.18b, I.20a, III.14c, III.22b, III.33c, III.93b

dyall: 'convey', pret. impersonal **diallad** IV.32b

dyar: adj. 'sad, sorrowful' III.51b

dit [dydd]: n.m. 'day' IV.12b, IV.19b, IV.22c, IV.31a

dyuot: 'come', vn I.28c, I.29c, III.55b; 3rd sg. pres./fut. ***daw*** I.11c, III.15b, III.16b, III.20c; 3rd sg. consuetudinal pres./fut. ***dyuyd*** III.21c; 3rd sg. pres. subjunctive ***dyppo*** IV.13c

dyuit [dyfydd]: n.m. 'grief, affliction' IV.34c

dyfrysyaw: 'hurry, hasten', 3rd pl. pres./fut. ***diuryssint*** IV.8b

dyffrynt, diffrint: n.m. 'valley' III.54a, IV.17a; in place-name *Dyffrynt Meissir* III.37b

dygredu: 'come near, visit, frequent', 3rd sg. pres./fut. ***dygret*** II.19c, II.20a

dygystudiaw: 'wear away', 3rd sg. pres./fut. ***dygystud*** III.25c

dyr: II.13a see note

dyrchafu: 'raise', 1st sg. imperf. conditional ***dyrchafwn*** III.98b

dyrein: 'rise, straighten', 3rd sg. pres./fut. ***dyre*** II.13c

dyry: see *rodi*

dywal: adj. 'fierce, furious', or as substantive n. 'fierce one, warrior' I.24a

e, f, ff

e: pron. see *i, y*

e: affixed 2nd sg. pron. representing *te* in *pereiste* IV.34c

ebyr: pl. of *aber* n.m.f. 'estuary' I.20b, III.38b

ech: prep. 'out of', ***ech adaf*** I.7b see note

echeidw: see *achadw*

echyuydei: III.64c see note

echwyd: n.m. 'place where cattle shelter from heat' III.55c
etlit [edlid]: n.m. 'longing, grief' I.21c, II.7c, III.20c
edrych: vn 'looking, observing' II.7c
edeweis: see *adaw*
edewit: n.m.f. 'promise, vow' I.9c
ef: 3rd sg. m. independent pron. III.35c, III.36c
efras: n.m. 'custom' III.52b, III.53b
ewur [efwr]: n.m. 'cowparsley' IV.15b
egin: collective n. 'shoots, buds, sprouts' II.7b
engi: 'escape', 3rd sg. pret. *egis* I.17c; 1st sg. pres. subjunctive *anghwyf* I.4c
ehut: adj. 'foolish, foolish person' II.18b
eidic [eiddig]: adj. 'greedy, desirous' III.40c–42c
eidigafael: 'injure, harm, tolerate, suffer', 1st sg. pres/fut. indicative *eidigafaf* III.66b see note
eidyl [eiddil]: (1) adj. 'feeble' II.13c, (2) as a substantive n. 'feeble one' I.14c
eidunaw: 'desire, long for', 3rd sg. pres./fut. *eidun* III.1d
eirmoet: adv. 'in my life, ever' II.16a
eiryan: adj. 'bright, dazzling' II.3a
eiryoet: adv. 'ever, always' II.1c, III.52b
eiry: n.m. 'snow' IV.5a–10a, IV.25a, IV.26b
eissillut: n.m. 'nature' I.20a
eleni: adv. 'this year' II.14c
eluit [elfydd]: n.f.m. 'world, land' IV.14c, IV.18c
elwic: adj. 'valuable, precious, profitable' I.3c
eleic [ellëig]: 'grey, grey-haired' IV.19a see note
emriv: n.m. 'sea spray' IV.16b
ennwir, enuir: III.8b see note, 'most faithful' IV.24c
erchwyn: n.m.f. 'bedside' II.5c, III.61c
erdywal: adj. 'fierce, warlike' III.77a
eredic: vn 'plowing' III.56c
eres: n. 'wonderful deeds, feats'? II.1b see note
eruit [erfid]: n.m. 'ebb, breakers, stream' I.21a
ergryt: n.m. horror, terror' I.12a
erniwaw: 'grieve for, lament', 1st sg. pres./fut. *erniwaf* III.62a

GLOSSARY

erwanu: 'pierce, stab, wound', 3rd sg. pres./fut. *erwan* III.33a

eryr: n.m. 'eagle' I. 20b, III.34a–44a; fig. 'hero, leader' III.58c

esbyt: pl. of n.m. *osb* 'guest' III.12b

escar: n.m. 'enemy' IV.23c

escor: vn 'casting off' II.21c

esmwyth: adj. 'comfortable, pleasant' III.24a

estrawn: n.m. 'stranger, outsider' II.15b see note

etiued: n.m. (1) 'heir, inheritor' III.47b; (2) 'progeny, issue' III.77b

ethiv: see *mynet*

eu: 3rd pl. possessive pron. II.15c, III.48b, III.49a, III.78c, IV.5c

eu: see *bot*

euan: III.41b see note

eur: (1) adj. 'gold, golden' I.11b; (2) n.m. 'gold' I.13b

eurdorchawc: adj. 'gold-torque wearing' I.25b, I.26b, I.27b see note

eurtirn: pl. of *eurdwrn* n.m. ? 'gold/ornamental mount' IV.11a see note

f, ff

ual, mal: prep. 'like, as' III.11c, III.85b

vi: see *mi*

fy, vy, uy: 1st sg. possessive pron. 'my' I.1a, , I.2c, I.18a, I.23a, II.1b, II.5c, III.27c, III.46c, III.66c, III.71c, III.86b, III.98b, IV.8b see note, *vym* I.4a, I.12b, II.16a, III.62c, III.66b, III.71a, III.78c, III.83a, III.100c; *vyg, uyg, vyng* I.29a, III.17a, III.48c, III.51c, III.69a, III.70a III.72c, III.80c; *vyn* I.29b, III.26c, III.46b, III.57c

ffaeth: III.46a see note

ffaw: n.m. 'fame, glory, reputation' III.86c

ffo: n.m. 'fleeing, flight, retreat' I.7c

ffoi: 'flee, retreat', 1st sg. pres. subjunctive *ffowyf* I.8c; 2nd pl. imperative *fouch* IV.30b

fonogion: n.pl. 'spearmen' IV.34a

ffraeth: adj. as substantive n. 'free-talking one, fluent one' I.7c

Ffranc: n.m. 'Germanic warrior' III.97c see note

ffruinclymu: 'tie by the bridle, tether', 3rd sg. pret. *ffruinclymus* IV.36c

phrydyaw [ffrydyaw]: vn 'brandish, shake, wave' III.97b

ffuc: n.m. 'deception, falsehood' *yr ffuc* III.86c 'falsely'

ffyd: n.f. 'faith' III.64c see note

ffisscau: vn 'attack, attacking' IV.23c

g

gadael: (1) 'leave', 3rd sg. pres./fut. *gat* III.23c; (2) 'permit, allow' 3rd sg. pres./fut. *gad* IV.8c; impersonal imperf. subjunctive *gattat* III.11a

gaeaf, gayaf, gaeaw: n.m. 'winter' II.5a, III.3a, IV.3a, IV.15a

gauael: vn 'seizing, grabbing' III.94b

gauyr: n.f. 'goat' III.69a, III.70a

gal: n.m. 'enemy; enmity; valour' I.24a

galar: n.m. 'grief' III.51c

galw: 'call, name', 3rd sg. pres. absolute *gelwit* III.38c, III.44a; impersonal pres./fut. *gelwir, geluir* II.9b, III.16c, III.43c, III.44c, III.78a, IV.19b; 3rd sg. fut. *galwawt* III.43a

galwytheint: adj. 'fierce in battle' I.28b

gallu: 'be able, be able to do', 1st sg. pres./fut. *gallaf* I.1b, II.19b

gan: prep. (1) 'with' IV.31a; conjugated 2nd sg. *gennyt* I.4c; 3rd sg. m. *gantaw* III.11c, 3rd pl. *ganthu* III.64c; (2) denoting agent 'by' II.6c, IV.21c; (3) in expression indicating personal feeling III.17a, III.66c; conjugated 1st sg. *gennyf* II.15a

ganet: see *geni*

garv: adj. 'rough, tempestuous' IV.16c

gaur: n.f.m. 'noise, cries' IV.12a

gen: n.f. 'mouth, mouthpiece' I.11b

geni : 'be born', impersonal pret. *ganet* II.14c, II.21b

glann, glan: n.f. 'bank, shore' I.9b, IV.16b, IV.21c

glas: adj. 'fresh, unbroken' II.15b; 'grey, green, blue' III.101b, IV.15b, IV.16b, III.53b see note; n. *glas y dit* 'break of day, dawn' IV.31a

glau [glaw]: n.m. 'rain' IV.16c

glew, glev: (1) adj. 'brave, valiant' I.28b; (2) as substantive n. 'the brave' I.6b, 'a brave one' IV.7c, IV.20c

gloes: n.f. 'agony, wound' III.101b

glvystec: adj. 'fair and lovely' IV.36b

glyw: n.m. 'lord' III.27c

GLOSSARY

gnawt: adj. 'usual, frequent, customary, common' I.7c, III.93c; comparative *gnodach* III.55b, III.56b

gne: n.m.f. 'colour, aspect' II.13a

gnif, gniw: n.m. (1) 'battle' I.5c; (2) 'battle, hardship' I.6c; (3) 'hardship, labour' II.21c; (4) 'tumult, contention' IV.18a

gnis: n.m. 'chin, face'; *ar y gnis* 'up to his chin' I.17b

gobryn: 'merit, deserve, gain', 3rd pl. imperf. *gobrynynt* III.86c

gochodi: 'afflict, sadden', 3rd sg. pres./fut. *gochawd* I.18a

godo: n.m. 'shelter, refuge, cover' IV.13a

godre: n.m. 'edge, tip' II.13a

godeith: n.f. 'bonfire, blaze' III.4a

govit, gouit: n.m. 'hardship, battle' I.21b, III.2a

govri: adj. 'noble, worthy, renowned' III.6a see note

gogaur: n.m.f. 'shelter, warmth' IV.12a

gognaw: vn 'provoking' III.94a, III.96a

goleith: n.m. 'avoiding, evasion' IV.13c

goleu: adj. 'clear, audible' II.6b

goleuat: n.m. 'light' III.20b

golo: n.m. 'cover, covering' IV.32c

golygon: n.pl. 'looks, gazes' III.80a, III.81a (emendation)

gordugor: n.m. 'condition, state' IV.22a

goralw: 'call loudly, call frequently', 3rd sg. imperf. *gorelwi* III.35a

goreu: see *da*

goreu: see *gorfod*

goreuynauc: adj. 'foam topped' IV.22b

gorfod: 'make', 3rd sg. pret. *goreu* III.87b

gorffowys: n.m. 'resting-place' III.45a

gorlas, guorlas, gvorlas: adj. 'very green' I.1c I.15c, I.19c, I.23c

goror: n.m.f. 'border, side' I.19b, IV.10a

gorthrymet: equative of adj. *gorthrwm* as exclamation 'how oppressive, how sad, how grievous' III.37a

gorsed: n.f. 'mound, tumulus, look-out point', as a common noun or part of the place-name *Gorsed Orwynnyon* III.80b

gorseuyll: 'linger, withstand, endure', pres. impersonal *gorseuir* IV.2c see note, IV.21e

goruchel: adj. 'very high, loud' IV.2b, IV.21d

goruit [gorwydd]: n.m. 'steed' IV.9b, IV.23a

gorwyf: III.105b see note

gorymdeith: 'go, travel, traverse', 3rd sg. pres./fut. *gorymda* III.39a

gosgubaw: 'sweep, make bare', 3rd sg. pres. absolute *gosgupid* IV.7a

gottoew: n.m. used as pl. 'spurs' I.13b

gran: n.f.m. 'cheek' III.93c

grudyeu: n.pl. 'cheeks' III.61b

gruc: collective n. 'heather' IV.22a

gryt, grid: n.m. 'battle, tumult' I.4a, IV.35a

gwae: interj. 'woe, woe is, woe to' I.21c, I.22c, II.14b, III.1d, III.21c, III.71c

gwaeannwyn, gwannwyn: n.m. 'spring' II.6a, III.4a

gwaet: n.m. 'blood' III.35b, III.38c, III.43b, III.44b, III.52c, III.53c, III.56b,

gwaedlyt: adj. 'bloody, bloodstained' III.48b

guaet [gwaedd]: n.f. 'cry' IV.21d, pl. *guaetev* IV.2b

guaetvann: adj. 'noisy, clamorous' IV.21d

gwaes: n.m. 'assertion, statement' I.14a

gwaew: n.m.f. 'spear' I.13c

gwall, gvall: (1) n.m. 'fault, negligence', *ar wall* 'disregarded, despised' IV.33b; (2) adj. 'lacking, wrong, evil'? III.85a see note

gwallt: collective n. 'hair' II.11b, II.12b

gwann, gwan, guan: adj. (1) 'depressing, sad' III.58a; (2) 'weak, sad' III.76a, IV.12a

gwanglaf: adj. 'weak and ill' III.62b

gwanu: 'pierce, kill, thrust through', 3rd sg. pres./fut. *gwan* III.27a; 3rd sg. pret. *gwant* III.3b

gwarthaw: see *ar warthaw* IV.7a

gwas: n.m. 'youth, lad' I.13a, I.14c, II.15a; double pl. with diminutive force 'little lads' *gweissyonein* I.27c

gwasgaru: 'spread', 3rd sg. pres./fut. ? *gwasgarawt* I.10a see note

gwaur: n.f.m. 'dawn' IV.12c

gwedy, wedy, guedy, uedy, guydi: (1) prep. 'after' I.2a, II.17b, II.20b, III.21b, III.23b, III.28b–31b, III.33b, III.49b, III.57b, III.58b, III.71a, III.72a, III.77c, IV.30c; (2) adv. 'afterwards' III.18c

gwed: n.f. 'shape, form' III.22a see note

GLOSSARY

gwehelyth: n.pl. of *gwahaliaeth* 'chieftains' III.84a

gueilgi: n.f. 'sea' IV.18c

gweirglawd: n.f.m. 'hay-field, meadow' III.91c, III.92a

gweissyonein: see *gwas*

guelet: 'see', 1st sg. pres./fut. I.5a *gwelif*; 1st sg. pret. *gweleis* III.33c

gueled: IV.18c see note

gwelit: III.38c, III.44b see note

gwely, guely: n.m. 'bed' II.17b, III.18b, IV.3a, IV.4a

gwell: see *da*

gwellt: collective n. 'grass' III.52c, III.56b

gwenn: II.13a see note

gvenin, guenin: collective n. 'bees' IV.12a–15a

gwenwyn: n.m. 'poison, venom, jealousy, anger, bad feeling' I.2b

gwerin: collective n. 'people' III.54c

gwers: n.f. 'while, turn' as adv. 'for a while' III.18c

gwerydre: n.f. 'country, land' III.1b, III.81b

gwgyd: n.m. 'warrior, attacker' I.18a

guir: adj. as adv. 'truly, certainly' IV.21e

gwisgaw: (1) 'arm oneself, put on arms', 3rd sg. pres./fut. *gwisc* I.6b, I.13b; 2nd sg. imperative *gwisc* I.2a; (2) 'wear, put on', 3rd sg. pres./fut. *gwisc* III.13b, III.100a; 3rd sg. imperf. *gwisgei* III.97a

gulip [gwlyb]: adj. 'wet, damp' IV.17a

gulybur: n.m. 'wetness, dampness' IV.15c

gwlychu: 'wet, soak', 3rd sg. pres. absolute *gulichid* IV.18b

gwneuthur: 'do, perform, make', 1st sg. pres./fut. *gwnaf* III.30c; 3rd sg. pres./fut. *gwna, guna* III.21c, III.60a, III.61b, IV.27a, IV.32; 3rd sg. pret. *gwnaeth* III.46b, 3rd sg. pret. *goruc* III.86b; 3rd sg. imperf. conditional *gunaei* IV.25b; impersonal pres. subjunctive *gwnelher* I.9c; *gwneuthur ar* 'inflict upon, commit against, bring about', 3rd sg. pret. *goruc ar* I.24b

gwr, gur: n.m. 'man, warrior' I.5c, I.6a, I.23a, III.13c, III.92c, III.98c, III.100a; IV.1c, IV.15c, IV.29a; pl. *gwyr, guir, gwir* I.28b, II.1c, II.5b, III.29c, III.35b, III.38c, III.43b, III.44b, III.50c, III.53c, III.63c, III.76c, III.77a, IV.23b, IV.35a

gwreic, gureic: n.f. 'woman' III.76a, IV.19c, pl. *gwraged* II.12c, III.29c

gurim: adj. 'brown, dark' IV.22a

gurumseirch: 'dark blue armour or horse trappings' III.79b

gwyal: n. collective 'saplings, shoots' III.85b

gwyar: n.m. 'blood, gore' III.34b

gwybot: 'know', 1st sg. pres. *gwn* III.91a; 3rd sg. pres. *gwyr* III.50c, III.104c, III.105c; 1st sg. imperf. *gwydwn* I.20a

gwych: adj. 'magnificent, noble, fine' III.12a

gwyd, guit, gvit: collective n. (1) 'trees, woods' II.13b, IV.4b, IV.7b, IV.11c; (2) 'masts, timbers' IV.10b; (3) 'timber, wood' IV.32c

gwydvit: n.f. 'forest; defensive enclosure'? III.2a see note

gwylat: adj. 'joyful' III.11b

guilan: n.f. 'seagull' IV.16b

gwylawt: III.43b see note to III.38b

gwylyaw: 'keep watch, watch over, guard', vn I.4b; 1st sg. pres./fut. *gwiliaf* I.1c, 3rd sg. pret. *gwelas* I.15a, *gwylwys* I.16a; *gwyliis* I.17a; *gwylyas* I.19a

gwynn, guin: adj. (1) 'white, fair' II.13a, IV.5a, IV.6a, IV.10a; (2) 'fair, fair-haired' III.13a, III.34c, III.47c; f. *gwenn* III.63a, III.64a; (3) 'blessed, happy' f. *gwen* III.21b, *gwynn y byt* 'blessed/fortunate is she' III.57a, III.58a;

gwynngnawt: n.m. 'white flesh' III.17b

gwynnovi: 'stain, splash, wallow', 3rd sg. imperf. *gwynnovi* III.35b

gwynt, guint: n.m. 'wind' II.13a, II.14a, IV.6c, IV.17a, IV.24a

gvir: adj. 'bent' IV.11c

gwirtliv [gwyrddliw]: adj. 'green-coloured' IV.14a

gvyrhaud: adj. 'bending, bent, bowed' IV.4c

gwythhwch: n.m. 'wild boar' III.9a

gyluin: n.m. 'beak' II.7c

h, i (y, e)

hael: adj. 'generous' III.94a

hawdit [hafddydd]: n.m. 'summer's day' IV.9c

hanuot: 'come from, spring from', vn I.3b; 3rd pl. imperf. *hannoedynt* III.63b

hawl: n.f. 'right, privilege' I.23a

heb: prep. 'without' II.21c, III.18b–20b, III.22a, III.24c, III.25b–27b, III.29c, IV.5c

hebawc: n.m.f. 'hawk' III.8a

hediw, hetiv: adv. 'today' III.15b, III.76a, IV.9c, IV.14c, IV.16c

hefyd: adv. 'also, in addition' III.109a

heint: n.f. 'illness' II.16c, III.60a

hen: (1) adj. 'old' I.1b, II.14c, II.17a, II.18a, II.20c; (2) as substantive n. 'old man' I.14c, II.8b, II.13c, IV.6b; (3) as epithet *Llywarch Hen* I.24c

heneint: n.m. 'old age' II.11a, II.12a, II.16c

heno: adv. 'tonight' III.18a–20a, III.23a–26a, III.28a–30a, III.32a, III.34a–37a, III.39a–48a, III.50a–51a, III.57a–59a, III.61a, III.62a, IV.27a

heul: n.m.f. 'sun' III.80c

hi: independent personal pron. 3rd sg. f. II.14b, II.14c, III.76c

hidyl: adj. 'copious' III.26c

hinon: n.f. 'good weather, fair weather' IV.17c

hir: adj. 'long' II.21c, III.80c, IV.16a; as adv. III.37c; comparative *hwy* III.80c

hiraeth: n.m. 'sorrow, longing' III.46c, III.81c

hiraethawc: adj. 'sad, yearning, nostalgic' II.8b

hoet: n.m. (1) 'longing' II.16c; (2) 'sorrow' III.35c, III.36c

hoen: n.m. 'joy, gladness' II.20a see note

hon: demonstrative pron. f. 'this' II.14a

hun: n.f. 'sleep' II.20a

hwn, hun: demonstrative pron. m. 'this' I.24c, IV.24c

hwy: see *hir*

hwyedic: adj. 'wandering'? III.78a, III.79a see note

hwyl: n.f. 'journey, course' III.80c

hwyr: adv. 'slowly' II.13c

hy: adj. 'bold' II.2a

hyt: prep. 'until' III.60b, ***hid in*** 'up to, as high as, up to the cruppers' IV.25a see note

hyt tra: conj. 'while, as long as' III.6c, III.11a, III.22c

hytwyth: III.24b see note

hyd, hit [hydd]: n.m. 'stag' II.13b, IV.4b, IV.17b

hynaf: n.m. 'lord, leader' III.30b

hynn: demonstrative pron. neuter 'this' II.5a

hint: n.f. 'path, way' IV.17a

hywed: adj. 'broken in, trained' III.72a

hywyd: adj. ? 'ready, skilful' I.16c

i, y, e: 1st sg. affixed auxiliary pron. I.4b, I.13a, II.9b, II.15a, III.17a, III.66b, III.69c, III.70c, III.91a, IV.25c

y, e: 3rd sg. m. possessive pron. I.11b, I.13b, I.16b see note, I.17b, III.3b, III.5c, III.10c, III.11b, III.13b, III.34a, III.39b, III.39c, III.40b–42b, III.45a, III.45b, III.84c, III.97b, IV.5a, IV.29b; with conj. *a* 'and' *a'e* I.11b, with prep *y* 'to' *o'e* I.26c, IV.5b

y: 3rd sg. f. possessive pron. III.21a, III.30b, III.31a, III.50b see note, III.52b, III.52c, III.53a, III.53b, III.53c, III.54a, III.54c, III.56b, III.57a, III.58a, III.76b, III.76c; as obj. of vn III.27a

y [MnW *i*]: prep. 'to, towards, for' I.13c, I.22b, I.23b, II.21a, III.11c, III.17b, III.47b, III.55c, III.69b, III.85c see *o*, III.92b, III.104b, III.105b, III.106c, IV.8b, IV.23c, IV.25c; with definite article *y'r* I.6b; with 1st sg. possesive pron. *y'm* II.11b, II.12b; with 3rd sg. m. possessive pron. *o'e* I.26c; conjugated 1st sg. *ym* I.8a, II.7c, *ymi, imi* I.16c, I.17c, I.19c, III.35c, IV.34c; 2nd sg. *yt* I.2c, III.12a; *y am* compound prep. 'from around, around' III.71a; *y ar* compound prep. '(from) on, on' IV.27c; *y wrth* compound prep. 'compared to' I.27c

i gyd: adv. 'entirely, completely' III.109b

ia: n.m. 'ice' IV.20b

iaen: n.f. 'sheet of ice, ice' III.3a, IV.4a

ieueinc: pl. adj. of *ieuanc* 'young', used as substantive n. 'the young' II.11c, III.1d

inneu, minneu: 1st sg. conjunctive pron III.101c; *a minneu* 'and as for me, and I' I.10b, III.51b

ior: n.m. 'ruler, lord' III.12b

ll, m, n

llachar: adj. 'bright, shining' I.4a

llad: n.m.f. 'liquor, ale' IV.32a

llad: 'kill, strike', impersonal pres./fut. *lledir* I.5b; impersonal fut. *lladawr* I.18c see note, III.65c; 3rd sg. pret. *llataut* IV.34a; impersonal pret. *llas* I.14b, I.23c, III.82a; impersonal pl. pret. *llesseint* I.29b, III.57c; in the phrase *llad celain/ celaned* 'strike dead, slay' 3rd sg. imperf. *ledi* III.7c

llauar, llauar: (1) adj. 'talkative' II.5b; (2) n.m.f. 'speech, talk' II.10c

llaw: n.f. 'hand' III.94a

llawch: see *llochi*

llawen: adj. 'happy, merry' III.54b

GLOSSARY

llauer [llawer]: 'many, many a' IV.10c, IV.20c

llaur: n.m. 'ground, surface' IV.18b

lle: n.m. 'place, room', *mudaw lle* 'give ground' I.6c

lleas: n.m. 'death' I.18b, II.20b

llef: n.m.f. 'cry, voice' III.34a

llefaru: 'speak, say', 1st sg. pres./fut. *llauaraf* I.8c; 1st sg. pres. subjunctive *llauarwyf* I.8a

lleuawr: adj. 'wailing' III.100c, III.101c

lleueryd: n.m.f. 'speech' II.8c

lleith: n. 'death' IV.13c

llen: n.f. 'mantle' IV.36b

lletkynt: n.m. 'sorrow, grief' III.87a

llethrit: adj. 'splendid, famous' III.44c

llew: n.m. 'lion' III.10a

llewa: 'consume, drink greedily', 3rd sg. pluperf. *llewssei* III.34b

lleuenit: n.m. 'joy, merriment' IV.32a

lliw [llif]: n.m. 'stream, flow of water, flood' IV.18b

llillen: n.f. 'nanny-goat' III.70b

lliw, llyu, llyw: n.m. 'colour' IV.5c, IV.17c see note, IV.36b

llochi: 'spoil, indulge', 3rd sg. pres./fut. *llawch* III.39c

llog [llong]: n.f. 'ship' IV.10b

llu, llv: n.m. 'host' I.24b, I.25a, III.6b, III.17c, III.64b, IV.25c

lluchedic: adj. 'bright, flashing' IV.11b

lludet: n.m. 'fatigue' II.21c

lluch [llwch]: n.m. 'lake' IV.3a

llvwyr [llwfyr]: n.m. 'coward' IV.10c

llum: adj. 'bare, barren' IV.1a, IV.10b, IV.16a, IV.20b

llwyt, lluid: adj. 'grey, grey-haired' III.40a–42a, III.14b, IV.16a

llwydaw: 'succeed', 3rd sg. pres. absolute *llwydit* III.39c

llyvrder: n.m. 'cowardice' IV.15c

llygru: 'spoil', 1st sg. pres./fut. *llygraf* I.12b; 3rd sg pres. absolute *llicrid* IV.1b.

llym, llem: adj. 'sharp, severe, penetrating' I.2b see note, I.4a, IV.1a

llin [llyn]: n.m. 'lake, pond, pool' IV.1b; pl. *llinnev* IV.5c

llyn: n.m. 'drink, liquor' II.5b, III.34b

llyri: pl. of *llwrw* n.m. 'path, track' IV.11b

llys: n.m.f. 'court' III.1c

llyth: adj. 'feeble, weak' III.84c

mab: n.m. (1) 'son' I.2c, I.16c, I.17c, I.19c, I.23a, I.26c, III.84c, III.94b, III.96b; (2) in patronymic I.24c, III.13a, IV.36a; (3) as diminutive in *mablan*; pl. used with numerals *meib* I.25a–29a

mablan: n.f. 'little enclosure, grave' III.47c

mat: adj. 'fortunate, good' as adv. prefixed to the verb 'well, worthily' III.13b, III.100a

magaud: adj. 'petted, pampered' IV.31c

magu: 'raise, rear, nurture', 3rd sg. pres. absolute *meccid* IV.10c; 3rd sg. pres./fut. *mac* III.77c; 3rd pl. imperf. *megynt* III.63c; 3rd sg. pret. *maeth* III.63a, IV.29c; 3rd sg. pret. *magas* III.84c; impersonal pret. *maguid* IV.28c

mal, ual: prep. 'like, as' III.11c, III.85b

malu: 'grind (to dust), 3rd sg. pres./fut. *mal* III.77c

mam: n.f. 'mother' I.2c, III.84c

man: n.m. 'mark, scar' III.93c

mann: n.m.f. 'place' III.65a

march: n.m. 'horse' II.15b, IV.36c; pl. *meirch* III.72a, III.78c, III.79c, IV.31c

marw: adj. 'dead' III.27c

maruar: collective n. 'embers' III.51a

mawr, maur: adj. 'great, big' I.18b, III.30c, III.33b, III.72b (emendation), III.101a, IV.6c

mawred: n.m. 'greatness' I.12b

medru: 'find, come across, hit upon', 2nd sg. pres./fut. *medrit* IV.26a

med, met: n.m. 'mead' III.69c, III.70c, IV.30c

medal: adj. 'soft' I.9a

medw: adj. 'drunk' III.69c, III.70c

meuil [mefyl]: n.m. 'shame, dishonour' IV.30c

meillyon: collective n. 'clover' III.48b

mein: adj. 'thin, slender' III.72c

meithyeint: n.m. 'begetting, nurturing' I.29a

melyn: adj. 'yellow' II.4b, III.61b, III.72b

men yt: conj. 'where' III.26c see note

merch: n.f. 'girl' II.15b, pl. 'daughters' *merched* III.107b

mi, vi: independent pron. 1st sg. II.11b, II.12a, II.15c, III.50c, III.65a, III.71c, III.108b, III.109b, IV.8c

migned: pl. of *mign* n.f. 'bog' I.9a

milgi: n.m. 'greyhound, hound' III.7a

minneu, inneu: 1st sg. conjunctive pron. III.101c, *a minneu* 'and as for me, and I' I.10b, III.51b

mor: n.m. 'sea' IV.10b, IV.14a, IV.22b, IV.35b; pl. *myr, mir* III.38a, IV.16c

mor: particle before equative of adj. in exclamatory construction 'so, how' III.11b, III.17a, III.57a, III.58a, IV.26a

mordwyt: n.f. 'thigh' I.19a, III.98b

morwyn: n.f. 'maiden' II.6c, III.13c; pl. *morynnyon* III.1a

mu hunan: pron. 1st sg. 'myself' III.27c

mudaw: with *lle* 'give ground', *mudif* 1st sg. pres./fut. I.6c

mwc [mwg]: n.m. 'smoke' III.91a

mwyn: adj. 'gentle, noble' III.106c

myuyr: n.m. 'memorial' III.53b see note

myget: adj. 'praiseworthy, honourable' III.37b

my hun: pron. 'myself' III.62b

mynet: 'go', 1st sg pres./fut. *aw* IV.8c; 3rd sg. pres./fut. *a* IV.5b; 3rd pl. pres./fut. *ant* I.21b, I.22b; 2nd sg. perf. *athwyt* III.22a; 3rd sg. perf. *ethiv* IV.30a; 3rd pl. perf. *edynt* III.85c

mynnu: 'desire, want', impersonal pret. *mynnat* III.96c; 3rd sg. pres./fut. subjunctive *mynno* III.2c; 2nd pl. imperative *mynuch* IV.30b

mynyd, mynit: n.m. 'mountain' III.66a, IV.10a, IV.18a

myr: see *mor*

na, nat: negative preverb, (1) before imperative I.2a, I.5c, IV.30b, IV.30c; (2) in subordinate clause I.8c, III.14b, IV.19c, III.87c; with 1st sg. infixed obj. pron. *na'm* II.19c; *nat* as copula in emphatic negative construction *neut nat* II.15c

na ... na: conj. 'neither ... nor' II.20a

namyn: conj. (1) 'except for' III.19c; (2) 'rather' III.62b

neb, nep: pron. 'anyone' II.19a; *yr neb* pron. antecedent to rel. clause III.23b; before n. 'any' IV.13c

new [nef]: n.f. 'heaven' IV.34c

neges: n.f. 'expedition, battle' I.22b, IV.5b

nei: n.m. 'nephew, first cousin's son' I.23b see note

neint: pl. of *nant* n.f. 'stream' I.10a

neithwyr: adv. 'last night' I.15a–17a, I.19a

nenn: n.f. 'roof, ceiling' III.21a, III.31a; 'upland, summit'? III.16a see note

ner: n.m. 'lord' III.24c

neut: affirmative preverbal particle before a vowel I.3a, II.10c, III.22a; with *ry* perfective preverbal particle *neur* II.4c, III.54c, III.80a, III.81a; with 3rd sg. obj. pron. *neu's* II.14a; with a negative particle as an emphatic negative copula *neut nat* II.15c; *neut* as copula in affirmative sentence II.4a, II.5a, II.5c, II.6a, II.7a, II.7b, III.1c, IV.18c

niuer [nifer]: n.m.f. 'host, company' III.24c

nywl [niwl]: n.m. 'mist, haze' III.91a

no, noc: conj. with comparative of adj. 'than' III.13c; III.56c

nodawc: ? adj. 'supportive' II.8a see note

nogyt: conj. with comparative of adj. 'than' III.55c

nos: n.f. 'night' II.21b, III.60b, IV.16a, IV.23c

nwyfvant: n.m. 'passion, vigour' III.105b

ny, nyt, nid, nyd: negative preverbal and relative particle, I.6a, I.8c, I.9c, I.12b, I.12c, I.14c, I.15b, I.17c, I.19c, II.19b, III.10c, III.15c, III.16c, III.22c, III.38b, III.50b, III.63b, III.63c, III.64c, III.65c, III.66b, III.84a, III.84b, III.84c, III.86c, III.87b, III.91a, III.97c, III.98b, III.100a, III.100c, III.101c, III.104c, III.105c, III.106c, IV.5b, IV.8c, IV.19a, IV.31c; before subordinate clause I.9c, III.13c, III.21c; with 1st sg. infixed obj. pron. *ny'm, ni'm* II.18c, II.19a, II.20a, IV.8c; with 2nd sg. infixed obj. pron *ny'th* IV.19b; with 3rd sg. m. infixed obj. pron. *ny's, ni's* III.36b, III.99b, IV.34b; with 3rd sg. infixed obj. pron *ny'w* III.100a; with 1st sg. infixed dat. pron. *ny'm, ni'm* III.72c, IV.25b, IV.32a; with 1st pl. infixed dat. pron. *ny'n* III.65c; *nyt, nid* negative of copula I.18c, III.13b, III.24a, III.59a–61a, III.96b, IV.9c; *ny* III.85a see note

nyth: n.m.f. 'nest' used figuratively III.84a

o, p

o: prep. (1) 'from' I.3b, III.16c, III.38c, III.55b, III.60b, III.71a, III.80b, III.81a, III.81b, III.85c, III.93b, III.106b, IV.20c, IV.23a, IV.29a; with contracted definite article *o'r* III.63b? see note; with 1st sg. possessive pron. *o'm* II.11b, II.12b; with the 3rd sg. m. possessive pron. *o'e* III.97c; conjugated

GLOSSARY 105

3rd sg. m. *ohonaw* III.96c, (2) 'of' I.13b, I.28b, III.77b; conjugated 3rd pl. *onadu* I.25c; (3) 'of' in adjectival construction III.106a, IV.29b, *a* I.29a, II.21a; (4) 'because of, from' III.4b, III.32b? see note, III.57c, III.100a; with contracted definite article *o'r* IV.32b; with 2nd sg. possessive pron *o'th* I.21c; with 3rd sg. f. possessive pron. *o'e* II.14b; (5) denoting agent of vn III.31b, III.49b; *o dv* compound 'on, beside' IV.9a; *o vn y un* 'one by one' III.85c

o: conj. 'if' I.5a, III.2b; with infixed 2nd sg. obj. pron. *o'th* I.5b; with 2nd sg. infixed dat. pron. *o'th* I.11c

o: interjection III.78b, III.79a; see also *o wi a*

och: exclamation 'alas' IV.19c

odit: n.m. 'rare thing, exceptional thing' III.2b

odi: 'snow, fall (of snow)', *ottid* 3rd sg. pres. absolute IV.5a–10a; *ottei* 3rd sg. imperf. conditional IV.25a

oe: see *y (i)* prep. 'to'

oet: n.m. (1) 'age' I.13a; (2) 'time' II.16b

oer: adj. (1) 'sad' I.15c; 'cold, sad' II.17a; (2)'cold' IV.3a, IV.4a, IV.5c, IV.11b, IV.13a, IV.14c, IV.17b

oeruelauc: adj. 'cold, chilling' IV.35b

oergrei: adj 'cold and sad' from *oer* 'cold, sad' + *crei* 'rough, harsh, sad' III.29a

oll: pron. 'everyone, all' or adv. 'entirely' III.85c; 'all' III.108b, III.109b

onnen: n.f. '(ash) spear' III.97b

onyt: conj. 'were it not, if not' III.101a

oric: n.f. 'short while, little while', diminutive of *awr* I.3c

o wi a: interjection 'oh, alas' III.23c

pa: interrogative pron. 'what' III.30c, IV.24c, IV.28c

padiw: interrogative 'to whom' III.78b, III.79b

pan, pann, ban: conj. 'when' I.6b, I.21b, I.22b, III.7b, III.9b, III.64b, III.97a, IV.13b, IV.31b

pan: interrogative 'why, how' IV.26c

par: n.m. 'spear' I.4a, II.3b, IV.29b

paradwys: n.f. 'paradise' II.2c

parch: n.m. 'honour, respect' III.29b

parhau: 'last, continue', 3rd sg. pres./fut. *para* III.50b, III.87b; 3rd sg. pres. absolute *pereid* III.87a

parth: conj. 'where' I.8b

pas: n.m. 'cough, coughing' II.16c

pedwar: cardinal number 'four' II.16a; *pedwar ... ar hugeint*: 'twenty-four' I.25a–29a

pedwardeg: cardinal number 'fourteen' III.79c

pedwarpwnn, pedwarpwn: 'four lordly'? III.104a–106a see note

pefyrbost: n.m. 'fair support' III.5a

peuyrbwyll: n.m. 'fine sense' III.6a

peithiawc: adj. 'ruined, devastated' III.28a

pelydyr: pl. of *paladr* n.m. 'spear' I.8b

pell: (1) adj. 'long, for a long time' II.10c; (2) adv. 'for a long time; from afar' III.43a, III.44a

penn: n.m.(1) 'head' III.3b; (2) 'top' III.24b; (3) 'mouth' III.97c; (4)'lord'? III.104b see note

penaeth: n.m. 'ruler' IV.29b

penngarn, pengarn: adj. 'tufted'? III.40a–42a see note

penntan: n.m. 'chimney corner, hearth' III.33c

perchen: n.m. 'lord, owner' III.104c–106c

peri: 'cause, make', 2nd sg. pret. *pereist* IV.34c

periw [perif]: n.m. 'chief, creator' IV.34c

phrydyaw: see under *ff*

pieu: 'own, possess', 3rd sg. imperf. *pieuat* III.23b see note

plant: n.pl. 'children' III.32b

pluawr: n. double pl. of *plu* 'feathers' III.72b

pop, pob: adj. 'every, each' III.65b, III.104b, III.105b; *pob awr* adv. 'continually, all the time' III.33a

porffor: adj. 'purple' III.12a see note

porthi: (1) 'bear, endure', 1st sg. pres./fut. *porthaf* I.6c; (2) 'support, assist'; 3rd sg. pret. *porthes* II.1c

prenn: n.m. (1) 'wooden object, stick' II.9c; gen. (2) 'of wood, wooden' II.4a, II.5a–10a; (3) 'tree' III.2a, III.16c

prennyal: n.m. 'spearfight' I.24a

priw [prif]: n.m. 'lord, chief' or adj. 'chief, foremost' IV.27b see note

prifgas: n.m. 'chief hate' II.16a

priffwch: n. 'attack'? III.9b

pryder: n.m. 'anxiety, concern' IV.27a

GLOSSARY

pwy: interrog. pron. 'who' III.19c

pwyll: n.m. 'sense, sanity' III.19c

pylgeint: n.m. 'cockcrow, daybreak' as adv. III.60c

pyscawt, pisscaud: n. sg. and collective 'fish' III.38b, IV.4a

r(h), s

rac: prep. (1) 'before' I.9b; (2)'against' IV.2b, IV.15a; (3)'because of' I.12a, III.101a, IV3a; (4) 'from', 1st sg. conjugated *ragof* III.86a

rann: n.f. 'party, side, company' III.65c

re: adv. 'swiftly' I.13c

redegawc: adj. 'running, free-moving' I.7a

redyn: collective n. 'bracken' II.4b

rei: pronoun 'some people, certain people' III.66c

reid: n.m. 'necessity, hardship, battle' IV.19b

ren: n.m. 'lord' IV.35c

reo, rev: n.m. 'ice, frost' IV.7a, IV.13b

rewi: 'freeze', 3rd sg. pres. absolute *reuhid, reuid* IV.1b, IV.6c, IV.13b; impersonal pres./fut. *rewittor* IV.35a

rianed: pl. of *rhiain* n.f. 'maiden' I.12c, II.19a

riw, riv: n.m.f. 'hill, slope' I.9a, III.15a, IV.9a, IV.14b, IV.16a, IV.26b

rodwydd, rodwit: n.f. 'ford' I.1c see note, IV.26a, IV.30a

rodi: 'give', 3rd sg. pres./fut. *dyry* III.19c; impersonal pres./fut. *rodir* III.78b, III.79b; 2nd sg. pret. *rodeist* III.3c; 3rd sg. pret. *rodes* I.11a; 3rd sg. imperative *rothid* IV.35c see note

ros: n.f. 'moor' IV.16a

ruch: n.m.f. 'garment, cloak'

rud, rut: adj. 'red, brown' II.4b, II.6b, II.7b, III.46c, III.48c, III.51c, IV.29b

ruthyr: n.m. 'rush, attack' I.20b

ruthraw: 'rush, hurry, attack', 1st sg. imperf. *ruthrwn* I.13c

rwng: prep. 'between' III.55a, III.56a

rwy: adj. 'too much, too great, excessive' III.46c, III.48c, III.51c

ruit: adv. 'easily' IV.26a

ruiw: n.m. 'ruler, leader' IV.30a

ry: (1) preverbal particle I.5b (note); (2) perfective preverbal particle I.14b, III.37c, III.43c, III.44c, IV.29c; with the 1st sg. infixed dat. pron. *ry'm* III.69c,

III.70c; with the 2nd sg. infixed obj. pron. *ry'th* I.22c; with the 3rd pl. obj. pron. *ry's* III.77c; combined with affirmative preverbal particle *neur* II.45c, III.54c; (3) preverbal particle indicating possibility (note) IV.1c, IV.20c

ry, ri: adv. 'too' IV.6c, IV.29a

rych: n.m.f. 'furrow' II.7b, pl. *rycheu* III.87b

ryt, rid: n.f. 'ford' I.4b, I.19c, I.23c, IV.1b, IV.13a, IV.26a, IV.35a

rydhau: 'free', 3rd sg. pres. subjunctive (jussive, expressing a wish) *rithao* IV.29a

ryhen: adj. as substantive n. 'too old one' I.21c, I.22c

s, t

sawl, y sawl: dem. pron. 'those' II.18c

sefyll: 'stand', *seiw* 3rd sg. pres./fut. IV.1c; 2nd pl. imperative *sefwch* III.1a; *sefwch allan* see note

segur: adj. 'idle' IV.6b

sengi: 'trample, tread on', 3rd sg. imperf. *sanghei* III.84a

stauell: n.f. 'hall' III.18a–33a

styllot: n.pl. 'planks, bier' III.17b

sich: adj. 'dry' IV.17a

syllu: 'gaze on, observe', 1st sg. pret. *sylleis* III.80a, III.81a; 2nd pl. imperative *syllwch* III.1a

tat: n.m. 'father' I.26c, III.5c, III.10c

tauawt: n.m. 'tongue' I.29b, III.46b, III.57c

tal: n.m. 'front, end, edge' I.9b, IV.20a, IV.21c

tan: n.m. 'fire' III.18b–20b, III.25b–27b

tande: n.m. 'blazing fire' or adj. 'burning, blazing' III.1c

tanc: n.m. 'peace, a truce' III.97c

tawaf: see *tewi*

tawr: 3rd sg. pres./fut. of defective verb 'bother, matter to' III.65c

techu: 'retreat, flee', 1st sg. pres./fut. *techaf* I.10c; 3rd sg. imperf. *techei*; III.84b; 3rd sg. pret. *techas* I.15b, I.19c

tec: adj. 'fair, fine' IV.23c

teneu: adj. (1) 'thin' I.1a, (2) 'biting' III.87a

terwyn: adj. 'fierce, ardent' III.106a

tes: n.m. 'warmth' IV.5c

teulu: n.m. 'troops, host, warband' III.26b, III.104b, IV.30b

tew, tev: adj. 'thick' III.87a, IV.7b

tewi: 'fall silent', 1st sg. pres./fut. *tawaf* III.18c

ti: independent pron. 2nd sg. I.14b

ti, (t)e: affixed pron. 2nd sg. IV.34c

tir: n.m. 'land, country' III.37c, III.47c, III.78c, IV.2a, IV.24c, IV.28c

tirion: n.pl. 'fallow land, uncultivated land' III.48a; III.80a see note

toet: n. sg. or pl. 'roofing, roofs' III.27b

toi: 'cover', 3rd sg. pres. absolute *toit, toid, tohid* I.21a, I.22a, IV.2a, IV.8a

tollglwyt: n.f. 'broken-doored' III.22c

tonn, ton: n.f. 'wave' I.7a, I.21a, I.22a, IV.2a, IV.22b, IV.35b

tonn: f. adj. of *twn* 'broken' III.55b

torri: 'break, tear', 3rd sg. pres. absolute *torrit* I.7b

tra: conj. 'while' I.13a

tra: prep. 'over, across' IV.2a

traet: n.pl. 'feet' III.53c

traeth: n.m. 'beach' I.7a

traha: n.m. 'violence, oppression' III.39c

trameint: adj. 'over-great' I.28c

tref: n.f. 'homestead, town' III.4c, III.5c, III.10c, III.43c, III.44c, III.83c; pl. *trewit* IV.18b; *tref tat* 'father's homestead, inheritance' III.95b

treidyaw: 'visit, go as far as, penetrate', 3rd sg. pres./fut. *treid* III.38b

tremynu: 'move', 3rd sg. pres./fut. *tremyn* III.61a

tridyblic: adj. 'bent in three' II.17c, II.18a

trigaw: 'remain, delay', preterite impersonal *trigwyd* I.3c see note

trinwosep: adj. 'battle-ready' I.6a

troetued: n.m.f. 'a foot, the length of a foot' III.84b

tru: adj. 'sad, wretched' III.17a, III.87c

truan: adj. 'wretched, pitiful' II.3c, II.17c, II.21a

trugarawc: adj. 'merciful' III.30c

truch [trwch]: adj. 'broken' IV.3b

trwm, trum: (1) adj. 'depressed, heavy of spirit' II.3c; (2) 'heavy' III.35c, III.36c; (3) n.m. 'battle' IV.20c

trwy, drwy: prep. 'through' I.29b, III.3b, III.16b

trwyn: n.m. 'nose' III.13b

tu, tv: n.m.f. 'side' I.1a, IV.2a; *o dv* compound prep. 'on, beside' IV.9a

tudedyn: n.m. 'blanket, cloak' III.72c

twll: adj. 'broken' III.14c

twrch: n.m. 'boar' III.3b, III.10c

tyfu: 'grow', 3rd pl. imperf. *tyuynt* III.85b

tyngu: 'befall, be fated', impersonal imperf. **tynget** II.21a

tynghet: n.f. 'fate' II.14b, II.21a

tylluras: adj. 'strong and stout' I.19a

tymyr: n.pl. 'lands, region' III.53a, III.62c, III.71a

tyrfu: 'thunder', 3rd sg. pres. absolute *tyruit* I.21a, I.22a

tyst: n.m. 'witness' I.14b

tywarchen: n.f. 'sod' III.77a

tywyll: adj. 'dark' III.18a–21a, III.25a, III.26a, III.31a, III.32a

tywyssawc: adj. 'princely' I.25b–27b see note

tywyssaw: 'lead', 1st sg. imperf. conditional *towissun* IV.25c

u, w, y

vch: comparative adj. of *uchel* 'high' III.66a

ugeint: cardinal number 'twenty', *pedwar ... ar hugeint* 'twenty-four' I.25a–29a

un, vn: (1) adj. 'one, same' I.3b, II.16b, III.16c, III.99c, IV.1c; (2) as substantive n. 'one person, one' III.15c, III.104b, III.105b; (3) cardinal number 'one' III.2a; *o vn y un* 'one by one' III.85c

unic: adj. 'lonely' II.17a

unben, vnben: n.m. 'lord' IV.19a, IV.36a, pl. *vnbynn* I.27b

vnweith: n. 'once'; *ar vnweith* adv. 'at once' III.83a

vi: see *mi*

vy: see *fy*

wedy: adv. 'after' I.2a see *gwedy*

wi a: exclamation of dismay, 'alas' II.19c

wrth: prep. (1) 'beside' I.15a, I.16a, I.17a; (2) 'at' III.54b

wy: 3rd pl. independent pron. III.46c, III.48c, III.51c

GLOSSARY

wylaw: 'weep, cry', 1st sg. pres./fut. *wylaf* III.18c, III.59c, III.60c

wyneb: n.m. (1) 'honour' I.5c, I.6a; (2) 'surface' III.52c, III.56b

y: 1st sg. affixed pron. see under *i*

y, e: 3rd sg. m. possessive pron. see under *i*

y: 3rd sg. f. possessive pron. see under *i*

y: prep. 'to, towards, for' see under *i*

y, i, yd: affirmative preverbal particle I.8b, I.23c, II.11a, II.12a, II.13c, II.14c, II.21b, III.11a, III.98a, III.107a, III.107b; with infixed 1st sg. obj. pron *y'm* III.23c, III.78a; with infixed 2nd sg. obj. pron. *i'th*, *y'th* II.9b, IV.28c

y, yr, ir: definite article 'the' I.11a, II.11c, I.13a, II.14a, II.21b, III.15a, III.16a, III.23b see note, III.29b, III.49b? see note, III.52a–56a, III.66a, III.70b, III.87b, III.92a? see note, IV.14c, IV.18c? see note, IV.26a? see note, IV.29a, IV.31; contracted *'r* with the prep. *y* 'to, for' *y'r* I.6b; with the conj. *a* 'and' *a'r* I.16b, I.17b, II.11c, II.12c; as a vocative particle *y* III.30b; with pron. *sawl* II.18c

y sawl: see *sawl* II.18c

ych: 2nd pl. possesive pron 'your' IV.22c

ych: n.pl. 'oxen' III.55c

yt, yd: preverbal particle I.15a see note, I.16a, I.17a, II.5b, II.16b, III.57c, III.78b, III.79b,

ytuo: III.65b see *atuot*

ydu: III.104c see note

yng: adj. 'constricted' III.47a

yma: adv. 'here' III.50c

imtuin [ymddwyn]: vn 'bearing, wearing' IV.28a

ymgyuyrdan: n.m. 'conversing, talk' III.33b

ymgynnwys: n.m. 'place of inclusion' III.45b

yn: possessive pron. 1st pl. 'our' I.3b

yn, in: prep. 'in, into' I.13a, I.19b, I.20b, III.9c, III.38b, III.53a, III.54a, III.100b, IV.16b, IV.17c, IV.19b, IV.30a; *y, i* (before *g*) I.4a, I. 21b?, III.2a, III.35b, III.53b, III.91c? see note, IV.12a, IV.13a, IV.18a, IV.35a; *y* (before *c*) III.35c, III.36c; *i* (before *m*) IV.18a; *yg, ig* (before *c,k*) I.28a, II.2b, II.6b, III.7b, IV.4a, IV.14a, IV.15a; *ym, im* (before *b,p*) III.9b, III.22b, III.52a, III.65b, IV.27a; *yn vn* 'in the one, at the same' II.16b; conjugated 3rd sg. m. *yndaw* I.11b; with contracted 2nd sg. possessive pron. *y'th* II.7

yn: 'as' III.95c, *yn was* 'as a youth', 'in the time of being a youth' II.15a

yn: with the vn III.4c, III.55b, III.83c, III.91b

yn, in: with adj. *yn wanglaf* III.62b, *yn vyw* 'alive' I.14b, III.71c; *in i bluch* IV.3c see note

yn y: conj. 'where' III.15b, III.16b

ynat: n.m. 'judge' III.95c, III.96b

yr, ir: prep. (1) 'despite' I.12a, I.15b, IV.13c; 'for, for the sake of' III.3c, III.98c; (2) 'by, through' III.86c

yr: conj. 'since' II.15a, II.21b

ys: see *bot*

ysef: demonstrative with the copula 'this is' III.52b

ysgaun: adj. 'light'

iscolheic: n.m. 'cleric' IV.19a

ysgwn, iscun: adj. 'ready, swift, strong, bold, stubborn' I.24a, IV.24b

ysgwyt, yscwyt, ysgwyd, yscuid: n.f. 'shield' I.1a, I.10c, I.16b, I.17b, III.14c, III.22b, III.55b, III.92b, IV.6b, IV.7c, IV.23a, IV.28a

ysgwyd, iscuit, yscuit: n.f. 'shoulder' I.16b, IV.6b, IV.7c

yssit: see *bot*

yssy: see *bot*

ystle: n.m. 'kind, kindred' III.93b

istrad: n.m.f. 'valley, plain' IV.8a

ystre: n.f. 'border' I.6b

ystywell: adj. 'kind, gentle, obedient' II.10a

www.ingramcontent.com/pod-product-compliance
Lightning Source LLC
Chambersburg PA
CBHW071510150426
43191CB00009B/1478